A Better Life

A Portrait of Highland Women in Nova Scotia

By Teresa MacIsaac

Cape Breton University Press
Sydney, Nova Scotia

Cape Breton University Press recognizes the support of the Province of Nova Scotia, through the Department of Tourism, Culture and Heritage. We are pleased to work in partnership with the Culture Division to develop and promote our cultural resources for Nova Scotians.

NOVA SCOTIA
Tourism, Culture and Heritage

Cover Design: Cathy MacLean, Pleasant Bay, NS
Layout: Mike Hunter, Louisbourg, NS
Printing in Canada by Marquis Book Printing, Cap St-Ignace, QC

Library and Archives Canada Cataloguing in Publication
MacIsaac, Teresa, 1935-
   A better life : a portrait of Highland women in Nova Scotia / Teresa MacIsaac.

Includes bibliographical references and index.
ISBN-13: 978-1-897009-17-8
ISBN-10: 1-897009-17-8

   1. Scottish Canadian women--Nova Scotia--Social conditions.
2. Scottish Canadian women--Nova Scotia--Social life and customs.
I. Title.

FC2350.S3M325 2006 305.48'891630716 C2006-906532-2

Cape Breton University Press
PO Box 5300
Sydney, NS B1P 6L2 Canada

A Better Life

A Portrait of Highland Women in Nova Scotia

By Teresa MacIsaac

Cape Breton University Press
Sydney, Nova Scotia

A Better Life
A Portrait of Highland Women of Nova Scotia

Contents

Preface

At some point in our lives, each of us yearns to know something of our roots. For many people, the urge comes too late and we are forced to interpret family lore through history books rather than by attending to the lived experiences of our forebears.

Being of Scots ancestry and having lived most of my life in the pastoral folds of Antigonish County, Nova Scotia, I have more than a passing acquaintance with what it means to be of Highland Scottish descent. I have long been struck by the grace and strength among the Highland Scottish women and the large numbers serving in the helping professions such as teaching, nursing and in religious congregations—often in some combination.

These are the undercurrents that became an inquiry into the lives of Highland Scottish women in Eastern Nova Scotia—an exploration of the traditions and experiences that shaped their lives. Our story begins in the 18th century, when a series of events compelled many Highlanders to travel across the ocean to a new life. It ends in the 1950s, by which time those Highland Scottish traditions that remained were becoming something to be cherished.

In order to understand more about the Highland Scottish women, it is necessary to explore the culture and traditions that shaped the society of their origin—the Western Highlands and Islands of Scotland—and that of the areas in which most settled—the eastern counties of Pictou, Antigonish, Inverness and Victoria. The largely oral culture of the Highlands made for strong memories and a tradition of preserving oral histories; these provided this account. This study has been contextualized by the knowledge and understanding of Highland Scots in Nova Scotia found in history books. The historical records support the cultural memory of those who lived it—the oral accounts and tales of the origins, traditions and experiences of Highland Scottish women.

To help to unlock this rich heritage, I interviewed eighty female descendants who knew the stories of the lives of early Scottish families in Nova Scotia. They had first-hand insight into the way of life of the Highland Scottish women which their family experiences and close affiliations provide. I also interviewed a number of sons who had similar memories and observations about their way of life. I examined these interviews and relevant documentation to determine how women saw their situation in Nova Scotia and what they were trying to achieve. This narrative is shaped from their point of view with relevant historical contextualization.

For background information, I used books, research reports, archival documents, government documents, journal articles and magazine and newspaper accounts. These sources were drawn from the extensive collections of documents available in the archives of Saint Francis Xavier University, the Beaton Institute, the Sisters of Charity, the Sisters of St. Martha, and the Sisters of Notre Dame. Valuable historical works that provided a backdrop for the women's experiences were obtained from the rare book room and the special collections of St. Francis Xavier University, the Antigonish Heritage Museum and the Museum of Industry in New Glasgow. I am especially indebted to the staff of these facilities for excellent service in helping me to access documents, particularly Sr. Margaret Beaton, Kate Currie, Sr. Marie Gillan, Jocelyn Gillis, Kathleen Mackenzie, Sr. Mary R. MacMullin and Maureen Williams. I also wish to thank Dr. Frances Hurley and Sr. Mary Olga McKenna for reviewing my manuscript and making helpful comments and corrections.

The map of Scotland is reproduced from Charles W. Dunn's *Highland Settler: A Portrait of the Scottish Gael in Cape Breton and Eastern Nova Scotia* with the kind permission of Breton Books. This and the maps of eastern Nova Scotia and Cape Breton indicate the locations of most of the places referred to in the text.

The idea of sharing this knowledge with my fellow Highland Scots has made the pursuit of this inquiry a labour of love. It was a pleasure to see how the fascination of this enterprise was shared by the people whom I interviewed. It was evident in the enthusiasm with which they related tales of their experiences and in the interest they expressed in learning more about the larger picture of which their stories are a part. It is my hope that this work will help to keep their stories alive.

The Highland Scots are noted storytellers. Their accounts contributed greatly to enriching my understanding of the traditions and experiences that shaped the way of life of the Highland Scottish women of this province and my own life. To the people I interviewed, I am deeply indebted.

T.M.

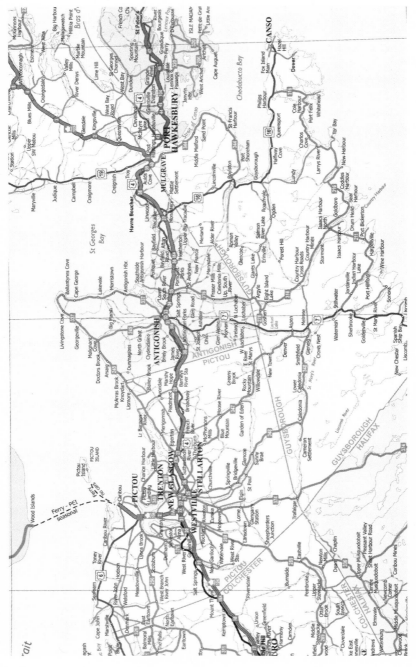

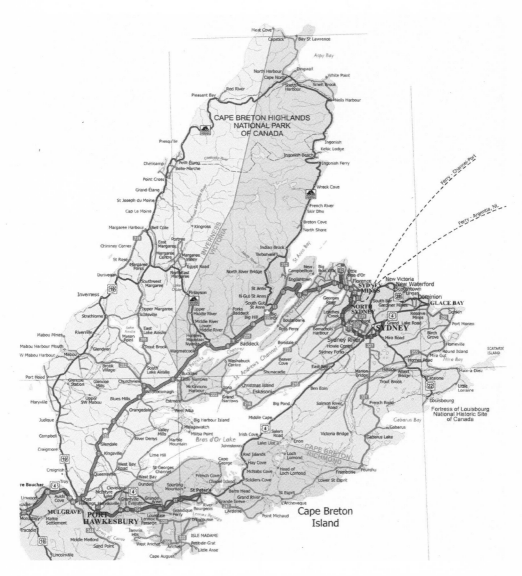

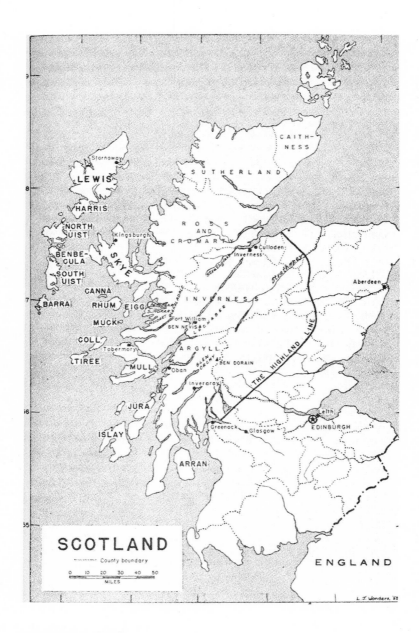

Courtesy Breton Books.

One

Upheaval in the Homeland

The story of the Highland Scottish women of Nova Scotia takes us back to their homeland, the shires in the western Highlands and Islands with place names familiar to Nova Scotians: Argyll, Inverness, Ross and Sutherland. They also came from islands in the Outer Hebrides: Lewis, Harris, North Uist, Benbecula, South Uist and Barra, and the inner islands of Skye, Canna, Rhum, Eigg, Muck, Mull, Coll and Tiree. As a largely oral culture, Highland and Island societies were deeply affiliated with their rugged landscapes. The beauty of the mountains, glens, lochs, rivers and the sea aroused closeness with nature and a love of their homeland.[1] The landscape fed their spirits, their emotions and their imaginations and was evident in their cultural expressions and appreciation of the Highlands' natural beauty. This appreciation for the land was transferred to North America when the settlers arrived.

The Highland Scots are a branch of the Celts who came from Ireland and who established their own Gaelic culture in Scotland. Their language was a dialect of the "Gaelic" branch of the Celtic languages, and the people who used this language called themselves "Gaels."[2] Along with language, the Gaels had their own literature and music;[3] their folk culture provides ample evidence that they were imaginative and artistically expressive. While outsiders may have thought the Highlands were bleak and forbidding, to imaginative Highlanders it was a source of delight and artistic inspiration.

The social system under which the Highland Scots lived was known as the clan system,[4] a form of tribal organization in which the land belongs to the entire group. The basis for this organization is hereditary by male descent,[5] and kinship and loyalty were its cohesive forces. Each clan was headed by a chief and subdivided into branches ruled by chieftains. For the most part, the chieftains carried out the will of the chief, but in military affairs they had as much influence. Clansmen owed military service and labour to their chief and, while the men were at his service, the women remained at home to do the work associated with their pastoral way of life.[6] This division of labour was based on tradition and necessity. Women were primarily responsible for the family's food and clothing, cooking, mending, weaving and sewing, in addition to tending the cattle and the sheep. Even though women did not directly serve the chief, they too identified themselves by the clan membership of their fathers, a source of affiliation that persisted long after the clan system was abolished. Clans feuded over land and raided each other's herds of cattle, making life harsh for everyone in the Highlands.

Scottish Highlanders were viewed by the English as barbaric and primitive and they were persecuted by English kings and parliaments for centuries. In the 16th century, the Scottish Parliament replaced the Roman Catholic church with the Presbyterian church as the official church of Scotland. The practice of Roman Catholicism was prohibited by laws passed in 1560, forbidding the celebration of mass in Latin, imposing harsh penalties on priests for performing the ceremony and abolishing the jurisdiction of the pope. For the remainder of the 16th century, parliament regularly passed additional legislation to undermine Roman Catholicism and the Gaelic language with which it was associated.[7] The enforcement of these laws waxed and waned, but even when they were not enforced, fear of them hung over the heads of Roman Catholic Highlanders.

The Gaelic tongue, still predominant among the Highlanders, was viewed as a mark of backwardness.[8] In its attempts to limit the use of Gaelic, the General Assembly of the Church of Scotland passed a resolution in 1646 requiring that an English school be established in every Highland parish, a policy made law by the Scottish parliament.[9] King William granted the rents of the bishopric of Argyle and the Isles for the building of English schools.

By 1698, there were twenty-five English schools in the Highlands and children were pressured to attend. Opposition to this affront had the consequence of drawing together Highlanders of all religious denominations to support the cause of the Stuarts, because their candidates for the throne were viewed as sympathetic to the Highlanders' desire to retain their language and culture.

To increase pressure to promote the establishment of English schools in the Highlands, a number of wealthy Lowlanders banded together in 1709 to form The Society in Scotland for the Propagation of Christian Knowledge (SSPCK).[10] They believed that ignorance and popery in the Western Highlands and Islands were largely the result of a lack of suitable instruction. Ostensibly founded to promote education in the Highlands, SSPCK instructional work was a front for undermining the Gaelic language and Catholicism. It established charity schools in the Highlands and Islands to teach the English language, Presbyterian religion, church music and arithmetic. These schools were Calvinist, anti-Catholic and anti-Jacobite.[11] By 1724, SSPCK had sixty schools in the Highlands and Islands.

The General Assembly of the Church of Scotland persuaded King George I to give SSPCK an annual grant of one thousand pounds,[12] indicating that the organization's work was of service to the state. The teachers in the charity schools worked as agents of SSPCK, commissioned to work on converting papists. To facilitate its work, SSPCK conducted an informal census of the small islands in 1764-1765, and people were classified according to their religious affiliation and their family status—husband, wife, widow, widower son or daughter.[13] This information gave SSPCK and the government agencies it served a more accurate sense of its target population. Efforts to undermine the Gaelic language and the Roman Catholic religion did not meet with much success, but did a great deal to alienate the Highlanders.

In 1745, Highlanders supported the claim to the English throne by Prince Charles Edward of the House of Stuart, popularly known as Bonnie Prince Charlie. The "rebel" Highlanders, were called Jacobites (after Jacobus, the Latin of James, for James the Pretender to the throne whom Highlanders also supported without success, in 1715). The Highlanders went to battle with the English army in 1746 and were soundly defeated in the Battle of Culloden. After the battle, the Duke of Cumberland, leader of the English forces, ordered contingents of his redcoats to "come down" on the rebellious Highlanders by land and by sea. Wives and mothers watched in horror as the redcoats butchered their husbands and sons as they lay on the ground in agony after the Battle of Culloden. The few to escape did so by fleeing to the surrounding mountains where they hid in caves. English redcoats searched the neighbouring towns, and terrified women watched as soldiers looted and destroyed their homes. Houses were burned with "rebel" clansmen deliberately locked inside,[14] and women and children were subjected to vicious attacks. Women thought to have pertinent information about clansmen were whipped and tortured; some were raped in the very doorways of their burning homes.[15] Children were put to the sword before their mothers' eyes, a fate that befell some women as well. Girls and young women were attacked by drunken soldiers. When the redcoats finished wreaking havoc on the homes and families of suspected supporters of the prince, they then turned their attention to the sources of the Highlanders' livelihood. They burned their crops and marched away with their cattle and sheep to destroy their means of sustenance.[16] These atrocities were not isolated incidents; according to one commentator, "Theft and pillage and rape and murder were rampant."[17]

The Highland Scots who came to Nova Scotia have never forgotten the cruel consequences of "the '45." Memories of the events were kept alive in the tales, songs, music and poetry of Nova Scotia's Highland Scots. Indeed, some of the people who supported the Bonnie Prince now rest in the graveyards of Canada.[18]

Margaret MacGregor of Upper South River, Antigonish County, a singer of Highland songs in Gaelic and English, spoke of the persistence of songs about the Battle of Culloden and its aftermath. According to MacGregor, one of the most popular of these songs is "The Skye Boat Song," which celebrates the bold effort of Flora MacDonald to ferry Bonnie Prince Charlie from the west coast of the Highlands across the sea to the Isle of Skye after his defeat. Another of these songs, "The March of the Cameron Men," has been passed down through the generations by the Camerons of eastern Nova Scotia. The song commemorates the march of the Cameron clan into battle under their chief, Locheil. Even today, some Camerons ask to have this sung at their funerals.

The absolute defeat of the rebels at Culloden marked a turning point in the lives of the Highland Scots. The British government reinforced the Duke of Cumberland's efforts to suppress the Highlanders and to prevent any further uprisings by passing legislation and implementing policies to undermine the clan system.[19] An Act for the Abolition of Heritable Jurisdictions was passed in 1748 to remove the hereditary power of the chiefs and force the chiefs who supported Bonnie Prince Charlie to forfeit their estates to the Crown.[20] These estates were to be administered by the Forfeited Estates Commissioner. Over time, persistent pressure to unify the Highlands under the English monarch had considerably weakened the clan system, but it took the removal of the hereditary power of the chiefs to bring it to an end.

With the abolition of the clan system, the value of a chief's estate came to be reckoned in terms of money rather than people. Chiefs who supported the British cause became landowners who now exacted rents instead of service. Under the clan system, tacksmen had served as military lieutenants for the chief in times of war and as his estate managers in times of peace.[21] In return they were given large leases of land, of which they and their families farmed part, with the help of servants, and they rented the remainder to sub-tenants. With the demise of the clan system these lieutenants were eliminated from the structure of estate management[22] and rents were raised to levels they could no longer afford. This was the main economic reason for the first great wave of emigration to North America,[23] where the idea of free land and a new life looked very attractive.[24] Those who chose to leave often paid their way by selling their cattle.

In addition to dismantling the clan system, the British parliament took further measures to undermine the culture of the Highlanders and to crush their independent spirit.[25] The Disarming Act, passed after the uprising of the Highlanders in 1715 in support of James the Pretender, was more rigorously enforced after the Battle of Culloden. Over and above requiring Highlanders to turn in their weapons, this law made it a punishable offense for them to own bagpipes, which the British viewed as instruments of war. The Unclothing Act of 1750 launched another attack on the culture of the Highlanders by forbidding the wearing of the kilt.[26] The indignation arising from these assaults on elements of the Highlanders' culture was added to that already festering from long-standing efforts to undermine their religion and language.

The largely Catholic Highlanders' support of Bonnie Prince Charlie was viewed as treason, and their defeat resulted in renewed religious persecution. While Highlanders believed the prince was their deliverer from religious and linguistic persecution, their activities on his behalf worsened their own situations. The renewal of religious persecution following the Battle of Culloden was marked by government orders to demolish all papist chapels and places of worship and to arrest all priests.[27] Priests were on the run throughout the Highlands; many took shelter in caves and dressed in lay clothes to avoid detection.[28] Practice of the faith by the laity was also outlawed; it was a legal offence to attend mass, to harbour a priest, or to make possible any gathering for worship.[29] The government urged Presbyterian ministers and their flocks to act as informers against Roman Catholics; most refused to do so.

The Catholic missions in the Highlands were far apart, separated by mountains, lakes and seas, and travel by priests was dangerous. Illegal masses were held in isolated homes that served as mass houses, guarded by clan members while priests secretly celebrated mass under the cover of darkness.[30] The enforcement of the penal laws denied Catholics access to the sacraments, and they smarted especially from the denial of their right to be married in their own church. It was galling for them to have the banns read and the marriage rite performed in the parish Presbyterian Church. Not until 1908 could a priest again perform the marriage ceremony in the Highlands.[31] For the most part, efforts to suppress the faith of the Highlanders were in vain. Sister Sarah MacPherson, a member of the Sisters of St. Martha, whose forebears suffered under these restrictions, took considerable satisfaction in expressing the view that religious oppression backfired: "It does my heart good to know that instead of undermining the faith of the Highlanders, this oppression only served to deepen their fervour."

"The Catholic pioneers came because of religious persecution," notes Florence MacDougall from Inverness County, words often repeated by the descendants of the Catholic Highlanders who came to Nova Scotia. Catholics left the Highlands in disproportionate numbers, given their representation in the total Highland population.[32]

After the failure of the 1745 rebellion, many of the Highland chiefs became at least nominal Protestants, but not all their previously loyal clan members were ready to follow them to the

Presbyterian church, known as the Kirk.[33] One of the former chiefs, the Laird of Boisdale, in 1770 began to persecute the Catholics of South Uist. As part of his campaign of religious persecution, he tried to force his Catholic tenants to join his Presbyterian congregation by herding them into the church with his yellow cane; as a result, Presbyterianism sometimes was known among the people of South Uist as "the creed of the yellow stick."[34] The Laird of Boisdale then summoned the three hundred families on his estate to a meeting where he placed before them a document containing a renunciation of their faith. They were ordered to sign or be driven from their homes. The people unanimously refused to sign; free land in North America and freedom from lairds looked more and more attractive.

Captain John MacDonald, Laird of Glenadale, moved by tales of the persecution of Catholics who supported Bonnie Prince Charlie, offered to lead the people of South Uist to land he had purchased on Prince Edward Island.[35] They accepted his offer and landed on Prince Edward Island in 1772. Disappointment with the landholding system prompted some of these immigrants to move on to Cape Breton Island, particularly to Judique and to East Bay.

Many families of the immigrants kept the stories of their exodus alive. Marie MacDonald, a descendant of one of the East Bay families, spoke with pride of the refusal of her forebears to renounce their faith, after she had visited their grave sites on Prince Edward Island. "The story of the 'religion of the yellow stick' and its impact on my people was handed down from generation to generation so that we would not forget the price our people paid for religious freedom."

Life got worse for the Highlanders who remained in Scotland. Many landowners decided they could make more money by raising sheep to provide wool for the textile mills in the south than by renting their land. By 1792, eviction of tenants to make room for sheep, which became known as the Clearances, was spreading methodically as more and more Highlanders were squeezed off the land their families had farmed for generations.[36] The evictions were betrayals and affronts to deeply engrained virtues of the Highlanders. Adding to their indignity was the ruthlessness with which some of the landlords and their hirelings evicted their tenants. The contempt the ruling classes held for the Highlanders could be seen in the deportations, many without consultation. Highlanders were treated "just as if they were slaves."[37]

The worst savagery may have been that wreaked upon the people of Sutherlandshire. Between 1811 and 1820, 15,000 people were driven from their homes. They were burned out and driven to the coast where they received 6,000 acres of poor land in compensation for 794,000 acres of good land.[38] The Clearances were often accompanied by brutality, and the landlord and his hirelings mercilessly ordered people out of their houses with no regard for age, sex or infirmity. Furniture and other articles too large to be carried away had to be left behind. In some instances the tenants were given but a half-hour to gather their meager belongings and get out.[39] Then the destruction began, with the landowners opening houses and torching them. Women cried aloud at the sight of the swift destruction of the homes they loved. The cries for mercy by pregnant women and children went unheeded. Those who were brave or foolhardy enough to stand in the way of the intruders were often beaten and sometimes killed.

It was the "cold-blooded murder" and the "senseless brutality" that accompanied the evictions from the land that made the later clearances so terrible.[40] Many evicted Highlanders had no choice but to sleep under the open sky, forced to exchange their crofts "for wretched patches among the barren rocks on the sea shore...."[41] Ruthless evictors even levelled the temporary shelters erected by the evicted; some people died of exposure or from resulting illness.

A few oppressed Highlanders managed to escape to the mountains to avoid deportation, but those who did not were dragged aboard ships to sail with unscrupulous captains who were known to dump their human cargo along isolated coasts in Cape Breton. They arrived destitute, and if there were no settlers in the surrounding area to help them, they likely starved. Often local settlers or natives came to their aid and if it were not for this assistance, many more would have perished in the bleak and inhospitable climate of this island in the North Atlantic.[42]

Witnesses kept alive the stories of the devastation and cruelty of the Clearances through stories that incorporate emotional reactions to the suffering of their people. This account of the reaction of a witness to the worst excesses of the Clearances survives in print:

... the expulsion of these unfortunate creatures from their homes—the man-hunt with policemen and bailiffs—the violent separation of families—the parent torn from the child, the mother from the daughter, the infamous trickery practiced on those who did embark—the abandonment of the aged, the infirm, women, and tender children in a foreign land—forms a tableau which cannot be dwelled on for an instant without horror. Words cannot depict the atrocity of the deed.[43]

The mass exodus of Catholics from the Highlands and Islands of Scotland eventually gave rise to a movement toward Roman Catholic emancipation. The British Government in 1829 passed an "Act for the Relief of His Majesty's Roman Catholic Subjects," which granted Roman Catholics freedom of worship, the right to inherit and purchase property and access to employment in the public service,[44] but the Highlanders were skeptical of these measures and they continued to leave. The gradual dismantling of laws restricting the rights of Roman Catholics enacted since the Reformation, was not enough to change their resolve.

In retrospect, one high-ranking British government official was willing to admit publicly to the terrible injustices that were wreaked upon British subjects. Reflections on the cruelty of the clearances moved the British statesman, Joseph Chamberlain, to make this speech in the town of Inverness in 1885:

The history of the Highland clearances is a black page in the account of private ownership of land.... Thousands of industrious, hard-working, God-fearing people were driven from the lands which had belonged to their ancestors, and which for generations they had cultivated; their houses were unroofed and destroyed; they were turned out homeless and forlorn, exposed to the inclemency of the winter season, left to perish on the hillsides or to swell the full flood of misery and destitution in the cities to which they were driven for refuge. In some cases the cruel kindness of the landlords provided the means of emigration—in some cases they were actually driven abroad. They suffered greatly in foreign countries, being without the means of sustaining themselves until they could earn a livelihood....[45]

In addition to these social, cultural and political conditions, the inability of the Western Highlands and Islands to support a large increase in population caused Highlanders to leave. A number of factors contributed to overpopulation in the late eighteenth and early nineteenth centuries.[46] The introduction of the potato, in the 1750s, enhanced the food supply and supplemented oatmeal as the dietary staple. Medical advances involving the widespread use of inoculation and vaccination against smallpox and other communicable diseases reduced the death rate, as did the cessation of warfare after 1746. New sources of income, such as the kelp industry, brought an improvement in the standard of living. Kelp, a plant harvested from the sea, was a source of alkali, a product used primarily in making explosives and fertilizer.

With these improvements the birth rate soared, creating a new set of problems, including the subdivision and subletting of land to the point where it could no longer produce enough food to support its occupants.[47] The problem of food production was at times compounded by crop failure. The potato blight of 1836-1837 and the complete failure of the potato crop in 1846-1847 brought terrible hardship.[48] The kelp industry collapsed in 1815 when kelp was replaced by barilla, a foreign substitute that cornered the market. Migration became an economic necessity.[49]

The Highland Scots' dream of a better life in North America was forged from the adverse social, political, and economic conditions in their homeland. As their lives worsened after 1815, "the deplorable conditions ... compelled many of them to clutch at the promise of the New World."[50] From adversity emerged the original strands in their dream, which varied somewhat with time and place. For tacksmen faced with rents they could no longer afford, for tenants forced off the land to make room for sheep, for tenants whose land had been subdivided to the point it could no longer support them, and for whom this problem was sometimes exacerbated by crop failure, the lure of free land in North America and the possibility of owning this land was very attractive. Years of oppression and persecution led to a general desire to be free, to be at peace, and to be safe. Highlanders who were subjected to measures to eradicate their language and those who saw their bagpipes and their kilts outlawed longed to restore these elements of their culture. Roman Catholics faced with religious persecution looked to the new land as a place where they would be free to practice their faith.

While Highlanders were victimized by conditions that turned their homeland into a hostile environment, there were also positive forces that engendered optimism about the possibility of achieving a better life in North America. One commentator argued that "the lure of real or fancied advantages in the New World did just as much as the disadvantages of the Old to induce the Highlanders to leave."[51] Some Highland soldiers who fought for the British in the Seven Years' War remained in North America and wrote letters home about the advantages of life there. Many Jacobites who had been banished to the American colonies immediately following the 1745 rebellion did likewise. Similar letters were written by representatives of shipping companies and emigration agents to promulgate seductive accounts of advantages in North America. The immigrants frequently made reference to these letters as a strong incentive behind their decision to come to Nova Scotia.[52]

For those who had a choice, the final decision to leave was usually made by the men—the women followed, sometimes reluctantly, but for the most part willingly. Some of them encouraged their husbands to make the decision for the family to leave. That wives often shared the sense of adventure with their husbands is evident from the stories they told their children about the crossing.[53] The willingness of large numbers of single women to make the voyage adds credence to the view that many women shared the sense of adventure and hope associated with the move to Nova Scotia.

Two

Crossing and Settling

The departure of the Highland Scots from the land of their birth
was traumatic. The pain of being torn from kinfolk and homeland
is captured in this news account published in the *Inverness Courier*
in 1841:

> The grief of the women was loud and open; clinging to the
> relatives they parted from, they poured forth, in almost unintel-
> ligible ejaculations, their agony at leaving the glens where
> they were born, and where they hoped to die, mingling in the
> same breath their blessings and their prayers for those whom,
> although they could never more see, they could never forget;
> while the children, stupified and bewildered at the scene
> around them, clung to their mothers and wept with them.[1]

Being left behind may have been harder than leaving, particularly
for the elderly. According to one witness, "These distressing farewells were not so impressive to my mind ... as the silent tragedy of
age. And remaining behind on the island were the bent old men
and wrinkled old women. They wandered back to their homes with
heavy hearts."[2]

After emotional farewells, the Highlanders boarded ship with
little awareness of the trials they would face. While there were
smooth crossings, far more were troubled. Few boats completed
the trip in the scheduled time of thirty days—many were blown
off course by storms, high waves and high winds, sometimes
doubling or even tripling the duration of a crossing. Some of the

ships on which the Highlanders travelled were well kept and had a sufficient supply of food, but conditions on others were terrible. Shipping agents were known to take advantage of inadequate regulations by overcrowding vessels. For example, the shipmaster of the *Nora*, which sailed in 1801, packed at least 500 passengers into the hold of the ship.[3]

Some Highlanders obtained passage on timber ships, ballast for the return trip to the colonies.[4] Overcrowding and the resulting dirt, disease, hunger, dampness, foul odours, combined to make many crossings dangerous.[5] Rotten food made passengers sick and too often there was not enough food to last for the entire voyage. Some passengers foreseeing or forewarned of these problems brought on board a cow to provide fresh milk. The passengers spent long hours crowded together in the dark under closed hatches below deck, and in these cramped quarters diseases such as small pox, dysentery and typhus spread quickly. They complained that because of the spray and the rain they were never dry from the day they left Scotland until they arrived in Pictou.[6] Women often had additional problems. Some gave birth in cramped and unsanitary quarters below deck, costing a few their lives. Children died in their mother's arms. The death rate for children was higher when epidemics broke out on ship; an outbreak of smallpox on the ship *Nora* in 1801, travelling from Fort William, on Scotland's west coast, to Pictou, Nova Scotia, claimed the lives of sixty-five children below the age of five.[7] A mother, reminiscing on the tragedy, told how the children

> were wrapped up in the narrow shroud of the dead, and placed
> in the sea without an elegy, without a lament, but only the
> heavy sighs of the mothers, and the bitter tears of the fathers
> and brothers and the onlookers who stood sadly around.[8]

The elderly as well as the young succumbed to illness—survivors weeping as they saw their elders dropped to a watery grave.[9]

One mythic tale of an Atlantic passage has been passed down orally from generation to generation. A descendant of an immigrant family, Christena MacDonald from Pleasant Valley retold the tale:

> The length of the crossing was increased by a vicious storm
> which blew the ship off course. The boat ran out of food, and the
> passengers were faced with starvation. The passengers included

a number of mothers with babies. The male passengers had a meeting and decided that rather than let the entire contingent die, it would be better to sacrifice the life of one baby. The women reluctantly went along with this decision. Each woman with a baby was given a stick, and it was agreed that the woman who drew the shortest stick would sacrifice her baby. The poor dear mother who lost the contest gave up her baby with great reluctance, and its life was terminated. The passengers then drank the blood of the child. The sacrifice of the baby enabled the passengers to sustain themselves, but they never forgot the terrible lengths to which they were driven to keep themselves alive.

The horrors of overcrowding on the transatlantic immigrant vessels brought about passage in the British House of Commons of the Passenger Vessel Act, of 1803.[10] This act specified the minimum space required for each passenger and regulated conditions to curb the worst excesses of the crossing. In the years following this legislation, shipping agents responded either by ignoring the new law or by raising the fare to cover the cost of additional space, food and medical attention that the law required.

For most immigrants, adversity continued after their arrival in eastern Nova Scotia. The Highlanders were ignorant of the land, its rigorous climate and difficult growing conditions. Most did not have sufficient supplies to survive their first winter and, in the first years of settlement, a good number of them perished from the cold, the wind and the vicious snowstorms. This was a climate more extreme than anything they had experienced in their homeland.

Pictou Harbour was the first point of entry for the immigrants from the western Highlands and Islands of Scotland, and the first large contingent of Highland Scots to establish a permanent settlement in eastern Nova Scotia arrived at Pictou on the ship *Hector* on September 15, 1773. While exact figures for the number of passengers are not available, there were at least 179 men, women and children on the *Hector*.[11] Most of these people came from the forfeited estates.[12] The *Hector* carried enough food for a voyage of standard length, but because it was driven off course by a hurricane, the passengers found that their food supplies were depleted long before the trip ended, and the discomforts they experienced aboard ship were soon replaced by the hardships of life in Pictou.

The only provisions that these families brought were some clothes, personal effects and a few supplies thought necessary for life in Nova Scotia. The new land looked so forbidding that some of the Scots wept in disappointment. When they learned that the land promised to them by the shipping company's agent, to lure them to Pictou, was already occupied, they refused to settle in the newly assigned land several miles inland. The shipping company's agent responded by refusing to give the immigrants the provisions the company had promised them and, in desperation, the men took their allotment of provisions by force from the shipping agent's store.[13]

Sixteen families, known as the Betsey settlers, were living in Pictou when the *Hector* arrived. These people had come from Philadelphia six years before the arrival of the Highlanders.[14] Their generosity quickly depleted their own supplies; it was too late in the season for the newly arrived Highlanders to start clearing the land to plant crops.

The Scots who remained in Pictou during that first winter had a difficult time. The Betsey settlers showed them how to build rough shelters from logs, spruce, boughs and bark, but these shelters did little to keep out the cold and the newcomers suffered terribly in that first winter.[15] Furthermore, the clothing and footwear they brought were not adequate to protect them from the harsh winter weather. Natives helped them hunt for deer and moose and showed them how to wrap themselves in the hides of these animals for protection from the winter cold and wind. Some traded personal possessions, others hired themselves out as labourers in order to obtain food.[16] While the men were away, the dense dark forests and the presence of wild animals made the women uneasy. Some of the women told stories of their wonderful journey across the ocean to their children to distract them from their fear.[17] The men usually returned with a bushel or two of potatoes and, in some cases, some flour that they carried on their backs or pulled on hand sleds.

Facing a bleak winter, the majority of the families decided to seek employment in Truro and the surrounding communities. They travelled forty miles on foot through trails blazed merely by axe marks on trees. The men and some of the women and children hired themselves out as labourers. Many women and children became indentured servants who did domestic labour and farm work.[18] Indentured service, a common practice in North America at that time, was a voluntary form of slavery in which the servant agreed to work for the owner of a household or homestead for a specified period in return for their keep, after which the servant was free.[19] Once the conditions of work had been fulfilled, the settlers returned to Pictou. Families who were not bound by service returned the following spring.

In the spring, the pioneers began the daunting task of felling trees to clear the land. An ax and a hoe were the only implements most of them had. Clearing the forest and planting the first crop was a joint project of the men, women and older children. The men cut the trees, while the women and children gathered and piled the brush, which was later burned. One recollection of the brush fires survives from the pioneer days in Pictou: "It was a great sight to see the fires burning in the early evening, and one could look across at the neighbouring hills, where the other settlers were doing likewise."[20] Ashes from the burned brush proved to be excellent fertilizer, and it was in the fertile soil around the tree stumps that the pioneers planted their first crop of potatoes. The Mi'kmaq taught the men how to hunt for deer and moose and how to fish through the ice over the rivers and the bay. This supply of game and fish improved their diet by supplementing the potatoes they reaped from their first crop. Natives also showed the men how to make and use canoes, which became an important means of transportation.

Once the Highlanders learned how to use the axe, the rich forests of Pictou County and the demand for lumber in Europe provided them with a way to work for cash. Access to cash enabled them to quickly improve their homes and their farms. The sight of ships leaving Pictou harbour loaded with lumber for the European market was a cause for celebration.

In the forty years following the arrival of the *Hector*, many more boatloads of Highlanders landed in Pictou. The first Highland settlement in Antigonish County was established at Arisag in 1791 and, as the population there increased, the Scots moved north along the ocean shore with pockets of settlements that reached all the way to Ballantynes Cove.[21] Later, a number of immigrants who had originally settled in Antigonish but were dissatisfied with the barrenness of the north-shore soil decided to move on to Cape Breton.[22]

By the turn of the century the shore land of Antigonish was occupied and the Highlanders moved inland along the rivers and the intervales. To make their way into the interior, they carried supplies on their backs and made a trail through the woods over Brown's Mountain and then followed the rivers inland. Over many of the rivers, logs served as simple foot bridges. Recalling the hardships of this journey, Sister Sarah MacPherson, a former resident of Upper South River, told of how her ancestors "carried live coals from Lismore over Brown's Mountain to the area where they would establish their new home in Upper South River, a distance of approximately forty miles."

The Catholics who went to Cape Breton made their first settlement at Judique. In 1801 several immigrants from Barra went to Iona, and shortly thereafter, other immigrants made their way to St. Peter's, Christmas Island, Washabuck and to the land surrounding the Bras d'Or Lakes.[23] The first group of Highland immigrants to sail directly to Cape Breton landed in Sydney in 1802.[24] The first Highlanders to settle in East Bay landed in 1812. The heaviest period of immigration to Nova Scotia and Cape Breton came after 1815,[25] as Highlanders were forced out by the Clearances and other forms of economic adversity. It is estimated that 19,000 Highlanders left Scotland between 1815 and 1821.[26]

Those who arrived at Pictou in 1815 were so destitute that the legislature of the province of Nova Scotia voted to allocate five hundred pounds for their relief during their first winter.[27] The influx of immigrants after 1815 continued to increase the population of Pictou County until it reached approximately 21,000 by 1838.[28] The immigrants who remained in Pictou and those who moved on to Antigonish and to Cape Breton would not have survived without the charity and kindness of the earlier settlers. It was reported that in Arisag "every log cabin was freely thrown open to all that might choose to share in the best cheer its humble inmates could afford."[29]

Between 1815 and 1838 the island of Cape Breton received the heaviest influx of immigrants, said to be "the poorest of the poor."[30] These immigrants landed primarily in Sydney and in Ship Harbour, later known as Port Hawkesbury. As before, unscrupulous ship captains sometimes dropped their passengers on coasts that were nowhere near habitation, leaving them, destitute and often sick, to go into the woods and fend for themselves.[31] Most of these castaways were unaccounted for in the official records. Sydney was the only place in Cape Breton where official records of arrivals were kept, and even these records were incomplete.

The population of Highlanders on Cape Breton Island rose from approximately 8,000 in 1817 to nearly 38,000 by 1838.[32] The Highland Scots quickly became the largest ethnic group in eastern Nova Scotia, outnumbering both the French and the English. By 1828, more than 13,000 Scots had settled in Inverness, and this influx of immigrants continued into the late 1840s. The final phase of immigration was between 1830 and 1850 and a substantial number of these later immigrants to Cape Breton located in scattered settlements of Victoria County including St. Ann's, Baddeck, Grand Narrows, Little Narrows, Bouldarderie, Middle River, Aspy, Bay St. Lawrence and Ingonish.[33]

Kinship and community ties, which were deeply rooted in the Highland way of life, played an important part in the migration process. "They eased the sorrow of leaving and provided an important source of support in the new land."[34] It was a common practice for families or individuals who knew each other to migrate together. New immigrants preferred to settle among people from their home district in Scotland, and they often named their new settlements after places dear to them in their homeland, such as Lismore, Arisag, Beauly, Inverness, Lochaber and Iona. Kinship and community ties sustained later settlers who arrived with few

Fig. 1 Lochaber homestead. Courtesy Antigonish Heritage Museum. 2003.053.023.

possessions. Many spent a year or two with friends or relatives before establishing their own homes. Settlers hosted the new immigrants for extended periods, and in many cases they also provided them with the seed needed to plant their first crops.

After 1827, settlers could no longer obtain land grants;[35] thereafter land was to be sold, not granted. Later immigrants did not have the money to purchase land and often had no choice but to become squatters on crown land that had not been previously settled—until they were able to raise enough cash to pay the modest sum required to gain clear title to the land.[36]

Just like the original settlers from the ship *Hector,* each subsequent shipload of pioneers faced the task of clearing the forest to make room for crops and dwellings. Out of logs they constructed crude one-room cabins with earthen floors,[37] filling the cracks between the logs with clay and making a hole in the roof for the smoke to escape and light to enter. The fireplace provided heat, light and a facility for cooking. Fire coals were kept alive day and night; if they did go out, the settlers would obtain embers from a neighbour. Food was cooked in an iron pot hung on an iron hook over the fire. Sometimes they roasted potatoes in the coals. Most of their kitchen utensils, including dishes, tubs, barrels and churns, were made of wood.[38] Food was served in rough wooden dishes. When dishes were not available, the family ate right from the cooking pot. Water for cooking, drinking and washing was obtained from springs and brooks. Spruce bows, and later straw that was dried by the fire, were placed on the floor to serve as beds. Their crude furniture usually consisted of a block of wood or a rough wooden bench which served as both table and chair.[39]

It did not take long for housing to improve. As early as 1803, the bark-covered, earthen-floored log cabins in Pictou County were replaced by larger frame houses or houses constructed of squared logs with wooden plank floors.[40] These newer houses had a large kitchen where the family lived and worked most of the time. A porch was sometimes attached to the kitchen providing a space for separating cream from milk and for churning butter. Many houses also had a parlour, which was used only on special occasions, such as a wake, a wedding or a visit from a cleric. Several small bedrooms provided sleeping quarters. Building frame houses depended on the establishment of a saw mill. Although some sawmills were in use in the early 1800s, they were not common until the 1830s.[41]

The diet of the original settlers consisted first of potatoes and later of porridge and bread made from oats and wheat, sometimes supplemented by fish and game. The settlers first obtained seed from neighbors or from a store in Pictou and later from their own crops. Oats and wheat were planted in the year following a potato crop. In the fall the men and the women cut the oats and wheat with a hand sickle, separated the oats and wheat from the straw with a flail and, before the proliferation of grist mills, ground it with a hand mill, called a *quern*.[42] In homes that did not have access to a *quern*, the women boiled the wheat in its raw state after its separation from the chaff. The centrality of oatmeal to the Scottish diet dates back to the invasions of the Romans around 80 AD when the Scots fled to the hills and lived on oats.[43]

Several generations of settlers relied heavily on wild game and fish until they were able to raise livestock. It could take several years for the settlers to clear enough land to support even a small number of livestock. Pigs were the first animals the settlers were able to raise because they needed less vegetation than other livestock to survive. Pigs got by on potatoes and fern roots found in the woods.[44] After clearing an acre or two of land, the steaders acquired a few sheep, in addition to the pigs, to provide wool and milk and, later, when more land was cleared and money saved, they got a cow. Before they had wool from sheep, many of the Scots grew flax, which the women spun and wove into cloth.[45] For many pioneer families it took years to clear enough land to grow the hay needed to feed a horse. As the settlers were able to grow larger crops, they traded the surplus for additional livestock and tools. Then, with the coming of livestock their diet expanded to include salt and fresh pork, lamb, chicken, milk, cheese and butter. A bit of luxury was added to the diet when the settlers learned how to tap the maple trees in the spring for syrup and sugar.

While the Highland Scots paid a high price for the pursuit of their dream of a better life, the results of their efforts made their pursuit rewarding. Even though life was hard, most tended to thrive in the new land. According to Frances MacIsaac of Brierly Brook, "The children of the settlers celebrated their ability to overcome adversity." Their desire to obtain land of their own was fulfilled and on this land they lived independent and relatively secure lives. They revelled in their release from oppression and in their new-found freedom to practice their religion, to speak their Gaelic language and to play their traditional music.

They lived close to the land and had a deep appreciation of nature. Their sensitivity to the beauty of their surroundings was a source of inspiration, and this appreciation of nature remained unabated among their descendants. R. S. J. MacDonald delivered a speech to delegates of the Scottish Society in Antigonish in 1931. Though a romanticized view of life in Nova Scotia, it reflects the nostalgia of many of the immigrants' descendants:

> But we shall show you the best we have—our own lovely unchanging country, our friendly mountains, fertile fields and eternal seas, that have given us, and those that went before, fuel and food, shelter and happiness. If you would stay for a little while amongst us, those of you from cities and towns could enjoy some of the sounds, the sights, and the smells of the country—the smell of the new mown hay as it is wafted up from the meadows, of the woodsmoke when the morning and evening fires are lighted, of the warm earth after soft summer showers, the sound of the babbling brooks as they sing their way to the sea, of the whetstone against the scythe, the distant sound of the wood-choppers axe, as it sings out in the silence of the frozen forest.
>
> The sight of a plowman coming over the brow of a hill, of the last load of hay going in at night by the light of the stars, the sight of a honking chain of wild geese as it wings its way to the southern skies. These are some of the things that are always with us, that strike down to the very depths of our nature and will go on to the end of time.[46]

Three

Culture and Language

Highland Scots are considered to be "peculiarly imaginative" characters.[1] Their art forms were inspired by the beliefs of the Celts,[2] and their culture was influenced by the wild and romantic aspects of the Highlands and Islands.[3] The Highlander has been described as "a dreamer, a poet, a mystic, and a romantic,"[4] and these characteristics too reflect the "spirit qualities" of the Celts. These same qualities came to Nova Scotia with the immigrants, and this cultural legacy is described as idealism derived from "their faith in God and the supernatural," as well as from "an exuberant imagination" animated by the exceptional quality of "their homeland, streams and forests, their hills and valleys. Their wealth of myth and legend they brought with them from the Old Land, and found in the new a ready grafting place for their legendary lore."[5]

The heart and soul of Highland Scottish folk culture was the Gaelic language. For the Highland Scots in the Old World and for their descendants in Nova Scotia, Gaelic, for the most part, was an oral language. The limited opportunity for education in Gaelic in the Scottish Highlands and in eastern Nova Scotia ensured that Gaelic would remain primarily an oral language. It was, therefore, prized for its expressiveness and as a suitable vehicle for capturing the spirit and the imagination of the people who spoke it.

The beauty and the power of this orality influenced imaginations to a degree that substituted clan memory and legend for formal education.[6] Because their literature enshrined their history, their aspirations and the great adventures of their heroes, it provided them with sources of ideals and inspiration. This literature was handed down from generation to generation by skilled storytellers who carried this tradition to Nova Scotia, where myths, legends and poems enriched the lives of the settlers as they struggled with the hardships of daily life.

Through recitation and memorization, the old tales were preserved and differed little from those told in the Scottish Highlands.[7] The listeners learned the tales and poems by oral repetition, and "the power of memory and fancy thus acquired a strength unexemplified among the peasantry of any other country where recitation is not practiced in a similar way."[8] In talking about the influence of the oral tradition, Jean MacPherson of St. Andrews noted that "to this day the Highland Scots have terrific memories." Through recitation the settlers also developed verbal fluency and good diction. In listening to the older Highland Scottish women of Nova Scotia, one is impressed by their facility for storytelling and their command of the language.

Before the arrival of Christianity in the 6th century, the Highlanders were pagans, and it is in pagan beliefs that the superstitious and the supernatural elements of their literature originate. Conversion to Christianity did not supplant their traditional beliefs and, for a thousand years, until the 16th century, Christian clergy ignored their pagan traditions. The influence of the realms of the supernatural and the superstitious were reflected in the Highlanders' tales of fairies, ghosts and witches, and in their belief in forerunners, second sight and the evil eye.

In the minds of the Highland settlers of eastern Nova Scotia and Cape Breton, fairies had a very real existence. Many of them held firmly to the belief that these creatures lived in the hills of the surrounding communities and that they interfered with their work. Annie MacDonald from Lismore recalled that "there was a widely held belief that fairies resided in the hills of Bailey's Brook." Fairies were often blamed for such misdeeds as souring the cream, thinning the milk and the disappearance of chickens.[9] Belief in fairies was so strong that it even became a subject for supplication in Gaelic prayer books. Celtic scholar Calum MacLeod was shown an old prayer book, still in use in Cape Breton, containing a petition for protection from fairies.[10]

35

In eastern Nova Scotia there were abundant tales of *bochdans* or ghosts. Highland Scots believed that *bochdans* were the souls of the dead who came back to do their purgatory here on earth or who returned to do something they had left undone. Tales of these figures of the imagination brought chills to the spines of listeners. The lore of the Scots also contained stories of the malevolent deeds of witches, whose dark powers were supposedly acquired from the devil. Belief in witches was widespread in the Scottish Highlands and in Nova Scotia, and they were often blamed for inflicting disease and bringing storms.

Stories of the evil eye and second sight abound. The evil eye was a folk belief connected with witchcraft. It empowered a person to inflict woe on others with the glance of an eye.[11] If put upon you, it could cause illness and misfortune for you or your family. People often attributed a streak of bad luck to the evil eye, and belief in the evil eye lingered for a long time in the Highland communities of eastern Nova Scotia. Second sight is the faculty of perceiving apparitions or phantoms that are associated with coming misfortune such as accidents or deaths. In its elementary form, it involves hearing strange noises or seeing light in unexpected places. In its strong form, it involves seeing apparitions of human phantoms associated with people living or dead.[12] Appearance of an apparition often indicated what was to happen to the person in the apparition. This faculty was viewed to be a great burden to the person who possessed it. Forerunners are related to second sight, but are more vague warnings of things to come.[13] Christena MacDonald of Pleasant Valley recalled that "a coffin maker who had this power would hear his tools rattle the night before he would be asked to make a coffin." Such forerunners warn of impending misfortune, but they do not indicate the person to whom it will happen.

To the Highlanders in the Old World and in Nova Scotia stories of these otherworldly events and figures were real. They helped explain the mysterious and the unknown, and they embodied their perceptions of the world. Because the folk tales were drawn so extensively from the realms of the supernatural and the superstitious, the Scottish Presbyterian clergy objected strongly to them[14]—objections that did not greatly mitigate the fascination of their Highland flock with these tales.

The subjects of folk tales in Nova Scotia included historical events of importance to the immigrants, such as the horrors of

Glencoe, Culloden and the Clearances, and the stories kept alive in their memories the injustices of these events and the bravery of the people in the face of them. An excerpt from a tale relating to the Battle of Culloden told in Arisaig in the 1930s illustrates the strength of the ties of the descendants of the immigrants to the 1745 Rebellion:

> Within a rifle shot from where I stand, in the old Arisag cemetery, close to the sounding sea, there lies sleeping the gentle Janet MacDonald..., daughter of the gallant, dark-eyed Captain Ronald MacDonald of Kinloch-Moidart, the first man in the Highlands to take up arms for Prince Charles.[15]

Bonnie Prince Charlie was the subject of many Scottish tales and songs, and in cultural terms he survives in these works, "not as himself, but as an ideal."[16] He was portrayed as a heroic, god-like figure because he was expected to be the saviour of his people.

Folktales composed in the Highland communities of eastern Nova Scotia and Cape Breton also recount settlers' memories of the adventures and hardships of their lives, including stories of the crossing of the Atlantic, death and burial at sea of women and children, meeting the Mi'kmaq people, clearing the forests, building their log cabins and planting their crops. These tales, transmitted orally, also express the Highlanders' delight in the beauty of their surroundings and the joys and sorrows of country life.[17]

The interest of the Highland Scots in their family ties goes back to the clan system when the chief of each clan had a bard who was an expert in genealogy and clan history. Genealogy was a topic of continuing interest in eastern Nova Scotia as the families attempted to keep alive the ties with their predecessors in the Scottish Highlands.

In a largely oral nation, poetry is the first vehicle of history, and the Highland Scots had a passion for poetry.[18] They committed to verse the deeds of their forebears and, through repetition, their traditions were handed down from generation to generation.[19] A remarkable specimen of such historical poetry is found in the "*Albanic Duran,*" composed in the 11th century. This long narrative poem contains the earliest history of the origins of Scotland, and a complete body of this history in verse is preserved in the poems of Ossian, a great Celtic bard.[20] The Ossianic sagas were perpetuated in the tales and ballads of the Highlands and were handed down by oral transmission from remote times.[21] The legends in these poems include the fascinating heroic figure known as Fionn, a great warrior. In the popular legends he belonged to a race of giants with superhuman power.[22] In addition, he embodied the Highlander's conception of the gentleman.[23] Calum MacLeod concluded that the values of the Highlanders were reflected in these tales and ballads. If a character "favors combat for the sake of glory, it favors it still more for the sake of fair play, for the element of danger, and for the attraction of the unknown."[24]

In addition to poetry, the inhabitants of the western Highlands and Islands of Scotland loved music. Their music was colourfully described as running "like a golden thread through the warp and woof of their lives. It was a second world to them, in which they roamed amidst delightful creations, all mirroring, as by magic pictures, the distilled experiences of their being."[25] The clan system fostered music as well as literature, and each chieftain maintained one or more musicians from the ranks of harpists and pipers.[26]

Even though musical composition was primarily the prerogative of the male, lyrics were also composed by women. In the Highlands, women were credited with writing beautiful poems and love songs and with inspiring those composed by men.[27] After the 1745 rebellion, passionate love became a subject for Gaelic poetry, and some of these poems were put to music.[28] Some of the best loved songs were actually composed by "broken-hearted maidens" who "learned through suffering what they taught in song."[28] Women composed beautiful lullabies to be sung to the children, and Josephine MacIsaac from Antigonish remembers "how her grandmother used to sing these lullabies in Gaelic." Women also composed *waulking* songs to be sung at milling frolics. *Waulking* is the process of finishing hand-woven cloth.[29]

In the Gaelic songs of Nova Scotia collected by Helen Creighton and Calum MacLeod, themes of love of the old country and of the new and the beauty of each abound.[30] These songs also expressed the woes and uncertainties of their eviction and immigration. Sister Margaret MacDonnell, a Celtic scholar who studied the folk songs of the Highland immigrants, concluded that most of them "even those which reveal the deep sorrow of the immigrants on leaving home, evince a strong urge to venture into a new and prosperous land and to enjoy the freedom and abundance to be found there."[31]

Folk songs were part of the daily activities of the Highland Scots who sang while they worked.[32] The rhythm of the song often supported the rhythm of the activity and added a pleasurable and sometimes humorous dimension to their work. They were said to have "songs for every occupation and every sentiment—war songs, boat songs, love songs, milking songs, *waulking* songs, *sheiling* songs, death songs, funeral songs, marching songs, marriage songs, nature songs, and religious songs and lullabies."[33]

Every Highland community in eastern Nova Scotia had its singers, bagpipers and fiddlers who brought joy to their listeners. Fiddlers were greatly appreciated because fiddle music was particularly well suited to dancing, and the playing of the fiddle and the bagpipes was the centrepiece of any Scottish gathering. Pipers performed laments at funerals and slow airs and dance music at weddings. Although most of the fiddlers and pipers were men, there is evidence of a few women musicians as well, and women were known for their fine singing.

Scottish Highland women did a great deal to keep alive the traditional folk crafts the settlers brought from the Highlands.[34] They perpetuated the crafts of carding, spinning, weaving, knitting and hooking by teaching them to their children. Long after the milling frolic ceased to be used to full the cloth, it was held in Cape Breton for the purpose of perpetuating the tradition. The *waulking* songs that accompanied the milling of the cloth contain a wealth of information about traditional life in the Highlands. The Highlanders incorporated the pleasures of music and socializing to ease the burden of work. The integration of folk arts and work gave them wide expression and appeal.

Fig. 2 An outdoor dance, Lismore, 1899. Courtesy Antigonish Heritage Museum. 2004.073.001.

The *Ceilidh*

The social life of the Highland communities in the old world and in Nova Scotia revolved around a social gathering known as the ceilidh, or a Highland house party. The traditional ceilidhs occurred "round the peat fires in the Highland cottage" where there "gathered on winter nights the tellers of traditional tales, and the singers of ancient songs, and the askers of cunning riddles."[35] A gathering of diverse talents in a warm home made for good story-telling, good music and good humour. The music of the *clarsach*, the harp, and later that of the bagpipes and the fiddle filled the house, and the young and old danced into the night. Often the women listened to the music and participated in the singing while they worked at spinning, carding, mending and knitting.[36] Traditional tales told in prose or poetry were favourite parts of the ceilidh. The storytellers who could best recite the heroic tales were most respected, and the listeners committed these tales to memory. Even in the Highland communities of eastern Nova Scotia, the old tales were preserved so faithfully that they scarcely differed from those that were popular in the Scottish Highlands. "Tell us a story, a story about the old, old days, about the Fein,"[37] a descendant might request, and the ancient lineages lived on in stories. The tales kept alive the great deeds of ancestral heroes as well as the supernatural and preternatural worlds. Gradually the range of their subject matter expanded to include tales of the Scottish settlers. Through the medium of storytelling the folk tales "provided the illiterate settler with a vivid and living literature."[38]

At the traditional ceilidh, men were the storytellers and the women listened and later repeated the stories to their children. Many descendants of Highland Scots reported that their mothers

Fig. 3 A helping hand from extended family. Hector *Exhibit Centre.*

were full of folk tales learned from their fathers. The obituary of Reverend Alexander MacLean Sinclair states: "From his mother and his grandmother, the poet's wife, he heard many of the stirring tales and songs of the Old Land, and acquired much of the history of the Highland clans and poets which stood him in such good stead in later years."[39] Beginning in the 1920s, the format of the Nova Scotia ceilidh gradually changed to include more emphasis on music, singing, dancing and card playing and less emphasis on story-telling. With this change in format, women began to play instruments and to lead the singing.

Lunch was a very popular feature of the ceilidh. In the 1920s and 1930s in Inverness County, the typical lunch included bannock, oat bread, wild strawberry or raspberry preserves, home-made cheese and strong tea.[40] The ceilidh remained the most popular form of social life in eastern Nova Scotia and Cape Breton until the advent of radio. In some rural communities the ceilidh evolved into the social, and the venue for this event was moved from the home into the school and later into the community hall. Socials enabled members of rural communities to come together in large numbers to listen to music, sing, dance, play cards and have lunch. The piano and accordion were added to the fiddle, and more and more women became fiddlers and performed at socials and community concerts. Community concerts were particularly popular at Christmas time; during the Advent season, preparation for the Christmas concert came ahead of academic activities in most rural schools.

Highland Societies were established as early as the 1860s in Nova Scotia to perpetuate and preserve the Highland folk culture and they continue to this day. In many eastern communities Highland Societies encouraged a variety of celebrations of Highland Scottish traditions, although many scholars today argue that these Societies were elitist and in fact have commercialized stereotypes that have been altered. The most widely celebrated events are Saint Andrew's day and Robby Burns day.

Calendar Festivals

For the Highland Scots the most important calendar festivals were Christmas, New Years and Halloween. In these festivals, elements of paganism survived, and in some cases existed side-by-side with elements of Christianity.[41] Christmas was originally a pagan winter solstice festival that became a Christian feast, and while it was a Christian observance in the Scottish Highlands, it never acquired the degree of importance that was attached to it in North America.[42] The religious dimension of Christmas was the most important aspect of the celebration for Roman Catholics in eastern Nova Scotia and Cape Breton, and the crowning event was the midnight mass to which many folks made their way by horse-drawn sleigh. Jean MacPherson, of St. Andrews, captured the sentiment of many Roman Catholics when she recalled past Christmases:

> I can still remember the sounds of the jingling of the bells on the shafts of the sleigh to the prancing of the horses' hoofs and of the crunching of the snow under the horses' feet as they made their way to church. We were warm as could be as we snuggled together under buffalo rugs to keep out the cold.

Many Highland seniors have fond memories of the traditional Christmas dinner: the birds oozing with aromatic stuffing, steaming mashed potatoes, mashed turnips, carrots and parsnips, sweetened with fresh butter. In rural communities in Nova Scotia, the twelve days of Christmas from December 25 to January 6 constituted the great season of social gatherings. Every home was visited by neighbours in the evenings, and the best food and drink were put out for the occasion. Annie MacDonald from Lismore recalled with considerable satisfaction "the great lengths to which the women went to prepare extra cheese, *maragan* and *isbean* for the enjoyment of the expected guests."

The custom of giving and receiving Christmas gifts did not come into vogue until the 1930s and the 1940s. Before that time the children hung their stockings behind the kitchen stove on Christmas eve, and the parents would fill them with fruit, nuts and candy—when they were available. Gift-giving became customary when female relatives working in the United States started to send boxes of gifts home for Christmas. The custom of having a Christmas tree did not become popular in the rural communities until the 1940s and the 1950s. Some descendants of the immigrants suggest that this custom was brought to the Highland Scots of Nova Scotia by their siblings and children living in the United States who observed the decorating of trees in the homes in which they worked. Before the arrival of electricity, small wax candles were placed on the Christmas tree, but few people risked lighting them.

In the Highlands of Scotland, New Years was the most important calendar festival.[43] Called Hogmanay, the celebrations began on New Year's Eve and continued into the following day. It was a great occasion for revelry in which all joyously engaged in visiting, eating and drinking. Even though celebration of the New Year is secondary to celebration of Christmas in Nova Scotia, the revelry surrounding New Year has continued.

The celebration of Halloween had strong pagan overtones, because it focused on the influence of the spirit world—an eerie celebration that filled people with awe.[44] Halloween provided an opportunity for good and evil spirits in the forms of ghosts, witches and fairies to wander at liberty through the imaginations of the believers.[45] Underlying this was a lingering belief in the power of the underworld and the occult. In Nova Scotia, Halloween was an occasion for hot-blooded foolery and trickery. Pranks that might land young people in trouble at any other time were tolerated, and mischief was often attributed to the work of witches and fairies. A treat known as *fourag,* a mixture of whipped cream and rolled oats, was provided to all takers, and youngsters bobbed for apples.

Rites of Passage

The main ceremonial events in the lives of the Highland Scots marking rites of passage were weddings and funerals. Weddings were formal occasions with rituals prescribed for every stage, from the marriage proposal to the wedding night. Practices for proposing marriage varied. Sometimes the prospective groom asked the woman's father for her hand in marriage; sometimes he asked a friend to do it for him.[46] It was not uncommon for this request to be made without the prospective bride's knowledge. The man might have seen the woman occasionally, and on this basis he decided that he wanted to marry her.[47] Once the father gave permission, the prospective groom then asked the woman for her hand.

The marriage ceremony was followed by a wedding celebration which was the occasion for at least a whole day and night of revelry. Fiddlers and pipers played joyous dance music through the night, and there was plenty of food, drink, music and dancing. In the late 19th and early 20th centuries in rural villages in Cape

Breton, the marriage ceremony was often followed by two receptions. The first was held the day of the wedding at the home of the bride; the second was held the next night at the groom's home. The practice of having two wedding receptions enabled the family and friends of newly-weds who came from distant communities to extend their visit and the celebration. On the night of the wedding it was a customary joke for friends and relatives of the newly married couple to gather outside their residence and make a disturbance until the couple came out and greeted them.

Wakes and funerals were solemn ceremonial occasions,[48] and wakes involved all-night vigils around the casket of the deceased. This practice grew out of the long-held Celtic belief that the soul stayed close to the corpse until burial. Because of the presence of the soul, it was not deemed appropriate to leave the deceased alone. All who came to pay respect were treated to food and drink. The social gathering and meal following the funeral, practiced to this day, is a carry-over from the Celtic tradition. The Highland Scots also believed that the departed spirits returned to their domestic abodes and influenced the affairs of the household, thus adding to ghost stories and belief in spirits.[49]

Technical Progress and Decline of Folk Culture

After the 1850s, the influence of the Highland Scottish folk culture in Nova Scotia declined because of gradual improvements in transportation and communication that broke down the isolation of communities and weakened cultural ties. Mail was the first means of communication that brought Nova Scotia communi-

Fig. 4 A gathering for a family wake, Keppoch. Courtesy Antigonish Heritage Museum. 2004.101.003.

ties in touch with the outside world. As early as 1815, mail was conveyed from Truro to Pictou by horse and wagon.[50] Mail service was extended from Pictou to Antigonish on a weekly basis in 1817, and twice-weekly service began in 1843.[51] Before the re-annexation of the island of Cape Breton to Nova Scotia in 1820, the mail was carried to Cape Breton by coastal vessels when the waters were ice free, often by Mi'kmaq couriers in winter.[52] From 1844 to 1852, mail was conveyed twice a week by coach between Antigonish and Halifax, and this service continued until the railway took over the mail service after 1880. Rural mail delivery did not start until 1908.[53] While mail service facilitated communication, its use was not sufficiently widespread or frequent to break down the isolation of the Highland Scots, as would occur with other means of communication and new forms of transportation.

Around 1850, the Nova Scotia government constructed a forty-five mile telegraph line between Truro and Pictou, which was quickly extended to Antigonish.[54] Telegraph offices were opened in both Pictou and Antigonish.[55] In 1856, the line from Pictou to Sydney came into operation. The Canadian Pacific Railway brought the first telegraph service to Stellarton and to New Glasgow the same year,[56] and it carried the Canadian Press wire news service. Until the coming of radio, the wire news service of the telegraph

Fig. 5 Mail wagon leaving Antigonish for Sherbrooke. Courtesy Antigonish Heritage Museum. 2000.026.002.

45

company was the primary source of news of the outside world. The latest news was posted in the windows of the local telegraph offices, and rural folks made a point of checking the news in the window when they were in town, then returned to their home communities and spread the news by word of mouth. People sometimes rode considerable distances to obtain news that they deemed important. A descendent of early immigrants, Annie V. MacDonald, recalled the story of how families in Maryvale, Antigonish County, obtained the results of the 1908 federal election:

> The only way to get this information at that time was to have someone go to the telegraph office. So the day after the election, a young man from the community jumped on his horse and rode into town to the telegraph office. Both the men and the women stood on their verandas to await his return, and being ardent Liberals, they were not disappointed. An hour or so later the young man reappeared and galloped through the community with his fist raised in victory.

The earliest newspaper in the area, *The Casket,* was established in Antigonish in 1852, and has been published weekly since that time. In deference to the Highland Scots, the type was half in Gaelic and half in English, a practice that continued for several decades. In 1892, a weekly Gaelic newspaper, *Mac-Talla,* began publication in Sydney, and this paper was probably the first regular Gaelic newspaper in the world.[57] Unfortunately, *Mac-Talla* was in competition with *The Casket,* and it ceased publication in 1904 because it did not attract sufficient numbers of subscribers or advertisers to survive. *The Casket* continued to have a loyal readership, providing local, provincial, national and international news. Even people who could not read anxiously awaited its arrival so that they could have relatives or friends read it to them.

The telephone facilitated faster and more generally accessible communication within and between communities. In the late 1800s and early 1900s, telephone exchanges were installed, and long distance service was available in eastern Nova Scotia as early as 1900. In 1878, the telephone was introduced to Pictou.[58] In 1887, the Nova Scotia Telephone company erected telephone poles throughout Pictou town and opened an exchange. Service to towns in East Pictou began in 1888 when an exchange was opened in New Glasgow. Two years later, the Nova Scotia Telephone Company provided reliable local and long distance services to Antigonish.[59]

Telephone service came to Marion Bridge in 1914, Margaree Forks in 1918 and Mabou in 1920.[60] Rural dwellers usually had a party line that compromised the privacy of their conversations.

The improvement in communication that had the greatest impact on bringing the Highland Scots in touch with the outside world was the coming of the radio in the late 1920s and the early 1930s. Because few people had radios during this period, neighbours gathered in the homes of those who did, to share an evening of listening. Listening to broadcasts of sports events was a particularly popular social occasion. By 1940, most homes had a radio, and in the early 1950s television service became available in eastern Nova Scotia. These media exposed the Scots to ideas and arts from other cultures, societies and countries.

The first major improvement in land transportation in eastern Nova Scotia was stagecoach service, and the first route was between Pictou and Halifax in 1828. The run continued until it was replaced by the Halifax to Pictou Landing railroad in 1867.[61] The first stagecoach service between Pictou and Antigonish began in 1833, and in 1851 stagecoaches connected Antigonish with New Glasgow through Marshy Hope. Travel was interrupted during the winter when the roads were blocked by snow and during the spring when the lowland roads were flooded or even washed out. In winter, the horse-drawn vehicles travelled on ice. Improved transportation was slow to arrive in Cape Breton where as late as 1839 there was no such thing as a wheeled vehicle.[62] The isolation maintained by the late arrival of improved land transportation helped maintain the Highland folk culture and the Gaelic language longer in rural Cape Breton than on the mainland.

Construction of the eastern extension of the railway leading from New Glasgow through Antigonish to the Strait of Canso was begun in 1877 and was opened for traffic in 1880.[63] Construction on the eastern line extension all the way from Halifax to Cape Breton was begun in the 1880s; by 1890 a rail line between Point Tupper and Sydney was opened. Steamers connected with express trains at the Strait of Canso for all points in Cape Breton. The coming of rail transportation facilitated contact with the outside world where English was the principal language and the predominance of Gaelic began to weaken. At the same time the isolation of the settlers was broken and transportation and communication improved lives, it facilitated mobility and an out-migration of the

Fig. 6 Preparing to rest stagecoach horses in Antigonish. Courtesy Antigonish Heritage Museum. 0099.

Fig. 7 Arrival of the stagecoach at the Caledonia Hotel in Antigonish. Courtesy Antigonish Heritage Museum. 91.47.

Highland Scots. It was by rail that men travelled to find mining work in Western Canada, Montana, Colorado and California, and women followed for jobs as teachers and nurses. It was by train and then steamer that most young Nova Scotia Highland women travelled to the New England States to find employment as house-keepers or factory workers.

The coming of the automobile in the early 1900s led to the development of better roads. When responsibility for highways was transferred from the counties to the province in 1907.[64] In the early 1930s, graders pulled by horses were replaced by mechanical equipment and in 1934 some roads were paved. Of course, paved highways were frequently blocked by drifting snow in winter.

The few people who had cars in the early decades of the 1900's stored them for the winter. Bad roads and mechanical problems made the early car a rather unreliable means of transportation until the 1930s and 1940s. Even though most women did not drive, the coming of the automobile brought the greatest mobility to the largest number of rural women as cars became more acces-sible—albeit usually through male relatives and friends. The car made it easier for rural women to have access to markets and it brought them into closer contact with urban environments.

Increasing contact with the outside world made the Highland Scots realize the pervasiveness of the English language, and a diminishing use of Gaelic was the hallmark of decline of the old Scottish culture in Nova Scotia. Because Highland women had more limited educational opportunities than men and because they had less contact with the outside world, Gaelic persisted longer among the women than the men—no wonder we call our first language the "mother tongue." Despite their love of the Gaelic language and despite the long-standing efforts of their forebears to retain it in the face of legal and educational efforts to eradicate it, beginning in the early 19th century, the Highland Scots ambivalently came to view the English language as an instrument of progress.

Fig. 8 Proud owners display an early 1900s car. Courtesy Antigonish Heritage Museum. 2003.115.002.

Fig. 9 Driving through Little River, Cheticamp, 1935. Courtesy Antigonish Heritage Museum. 2004.056.013.

In the interest of the advancement of their children toward better lives, they made a deliberate effort to abstain from using Gaelic in front of them and often did not teach their children to speak it. The Highland Scots' vision of a better life was now influenced by forces outside their traditional culture.

Gaelic declined first on the mainland of eastern Nova Scotia and then several decades later in Cape Breton.[65] This decline was followed somewhat later by a decline of the folk arts. Highland Scottish folk culture gradually weakened until by the late 1950s it was becoming more a tradition to cherish than an active flourishing expression of a distinctive way of life. As the folk culture declined, a permanent institution, known as the Gaelic College, was established in 1939 at St. Ann's, Cape Breton, to perpetuate and promote Highland arts and crafts.[66] The college still offers summer schools on campus and extension courses during the winter. Its programs include the Gaelic language, Gaelic singing, bagpipe music, Scottish folk singing and dancing, clan lore and the weaving of plaids and tartans. The college also started an annual summer celebration of the Highland folk culture known as the Gaelic Mod. St. Francis Xavier University in Antigonish started a program in Celtic Studies in 1958 that offered courses in Gaelic, Celtic history and Celtic literature.[67] The university was founded by Highland Scots and this tradition made it important for the university to preserve their cultural legacy.

Four

Religion

Religion was central to the lives of the Highland Scottish women of eastern Nova Scotia and Cape Breton. Their faith was a precious possession and they were noted for devotion to their churches. For the most part, Nova Scotia Scots were either Presbyterian or Roman Catholic; both denominations gave high priority to spiritual values.

The religious fervour of the Highland women had roots deep in the past. Prior to the coming of Christianity, the people of the Highlands and Islands of Scotland were pagan, enchanted with the realms of the supernatural and the superstitious. The early Christian missionaries decided not to interfere with the Highlanders' pagan beliefs,[1] and their success in converting the Highland Scots to Christianity may be partially attributed to their willingness to let the two sets of beliefs coexist. Allegiance to a mix of pagan and Christian beliefs was prevalent. The continuation of this spiritual duality in Nova Scotia was reflected in the interest of even the most devout settlers with the superstitious and the supernatural realms.

Presbyterians

The first Highland Scottish settlers of Eastern Nova Scotia were the passengers from the ship *Hector* that arrived at Pictou in 1773. They were almost all Presbyterians. Their faith and liturgy were based in the Scottish Reform Church of John Knox and they were distinctive by preaching the Word in Gaelic (only later in English), administration of the sacraments and strict moral discipline.[2] Church services were conducted by ministers and all other church functions were exercised by lay persons. Each congregation had deacons who served as financial officers and elders who looked after the exercise of discipline and later took over all the administrative work of the church. Presbyterian church buildings were simple and unadorned to the point of being bleak.[3] Church ornamentation was frowned upon because it detracted from contemplation of the spirit. The early Scottish Presbyterians believed that God was a spirit and should be worshipped only in spirit.

The Scottish Reform Church of John Knox placed a strong emphasis on Calvinism and this tradition was pervasive among the Presbyterians who came to eastern Nova Scotia. The Calvinist emphasis on personal responsibility manifested itself in the "Protestant work ethic."[4] Young people grew up with the idea that they were to develop their God-given talents to the best of their ability. The result was that many of the small rural communities in which the Presbyterian Scots lived produced a remarkably large number of ministers, lawyers, doctors and politicians, many of whom achieved wide recognition for their outstanding achievements. Elderly Highland Scots reported that their mothers, some-

Fig. 10 Replica of the first Presbyterian church in Pictou County (Loch Broom, 1787). Hector *Exhibit Centre.*

times even more than their fathers, emphasized the importance of an education. Vera Williams, a Presbyterian Scot from Antigonish, recalled the story of one of her female relatives "who walked with her son all the way to Truro following a blaze through the woods to make arrangements for him to get an education in a Presbyterian setting."

Pictou was the cradle of Presbyterianism in Nova Scotia. In the early days of the settlement at Pictou there was no permanent clergy; visiting ministers came to Pictou in the summer and stayed a week or more to serve the settlers. Some faithful settlers walked forty miles through the woods to Truro for the annual communion service and carried their babies with them to be baptized.[5] During the greater part of the year when the people did not have the services of a minister, those who wished to worship met on Sundays for prayer, praise and scripture reading. Many families worshipped daily through morning and evening prayers, Bible reading and blessings at meals. A decade after the arrival of the *Hector*, the population of Pictou had increased sufficiently to support a full-time minister and they petitioned the General Synod of the Church of Scotland requesting the services of one.[6] Rev. James MacGregor arrived in 1786. He found his assignment to be challenging because his services extended to all of the settlements in Pictou County and on a mission basis to other parts of eastern Nova Scotia. His parishioners' captivation with superstitious beliefs was something he may not have fully anticipated. The pervasiveness of their beliefs in witches, fairies and *bochdans*, and the hold of these otherworldly figures on them, indicated the degree to which the Christians whom he served held to their old-world beliefs.

The Presbyterian Church that developed in eastern Nova Scotia was predominantly Scottish in its origin, traditions and loyalties,[7] and its identification with the Scottish tradition continued into the 20th century. Many Presbyterian Scots in the Highlands who had become dissatisfied with the original Presbyterian Church of Scotland and seceded, and divisions within the Kirk in Scotland had their counterparts in Nova Scotia.[8] The first break was by the Secessionists over the question of a voice for the people in the selection of ministers. In Pictou County there was contention between Secessionists and Kirkmen. Rev. James MacGregor was a representative of the Secessionist branch, and the differences between his church and the Kirk, of which many of the immigrants were members, divided Presbyterians in Pictou County for years. Divisiveness among Presbyterians was flamed by "the Kirk's assumption of its own superiority over all other branches of Presbyterianism, and especially over colonial branches."[9] These differences were resolved and the two churches united in 1860.

Regularized formal church services began in Cape Breton around 1833. The only contact the Presbyterian Scots in Cape Breton had with clergy prior to this was an occasional visit from Rev. MacGregor who made his first trip to Cape Breton in 1798. At that time there were only about twenty Presbyterian families in Cape Breton, and none of them were Highland Scots. In 1802, a stream of Presbyterian immigrants from the Highlands and Islands of Scotland began to flow into Inverness County and this flow continued for almost half a century. By 1861, there were approximately 23,655 Presbyterians in Cape Breton.[10] Religious beliefs of the immigrants who settled in Cape Breton before 1825 reflected the views of the moderates who in the early 18th century attempted to modernize the Presbyterian Church of Scotland. Relaxation of the enforcement of discipline and puritanical values resulted in a level of indifference to the church.[11] These immigrants were untouched by the evangelical fervour that spread through the Highlands in the 1820s.[12]

From the middle of the 1820s through the 1830s, devout Calvinists began to arrive in Cape Breton and they sought to reverse the secular trend promoted by the moderate Presbyterians who had arrived before them. For the Calvinists, self denial was important, and they renounced the joyousness of bagpipes, fiddles, dancing, storytelling and alcohol. They were devoted to Bible reading and family prayer and they strictly observed the Sabbath as a day of rest and religiosity.[13] For this group and their successors for generations to come, Sunday was reserved as a day of worship. Lorne MacLellan of Sydney Mines described the strictness of their Sunday observances: "There was to be no work of any kind that could be avoided. All food for Sunday was to be prepared on Saturday, and even the clothes to be worn to Sunday services were to be laid out on the previous evening. Sunday was a day for going to church, for attending Sunday school, and for religious reading."

The religious revival in Cape Breton can be attributed in part to a missionary society in Scotland known as the Edinburgh Ladies Association, which made Cape Breton its mission.[14] As a result of the efforts of their leader, Isabella MacKay, this organization raised the money to cover the expenses of a minister for Cape Breton. MacKay then spearheaded efforts to supply each parish on the island with clergy and two schoolmasters. Perhaps just as important as the work of the missionary society in bringing the church to the people was the part this organization played in drawing attention to the plight of the immigrants.[15] It became the most important agency in assisting Cape Breton Presbyterian settlers to adapt to their new home.

The cleric who is credited with being the most dynamic force behind the Presbyterian revival in Cape Breton was Rev. Peter MacLean.[16] In the 1840s, his efforts resulted in kindling an eager desire for religious instruction and evangelism in half a dozen communities. The annual communion service was an important part of the heritage of the Presbyterian Scots. Rev. MacLean's ability to draw people to this service is illustrated by a local newspaper article by a correspondent who witnessed a communion service at Whycocomagh, where, according to his report, there were "two hundred boats anchored in the bay and five hundred horses tied in the woods."[17] The communion service was an ecclesiastical celebration the Highlanders brought from Scotland.[18] It was considered so important to the lives of the Presbyterian Scots in Cape Breton that some of them sailed or rode forty to fifty miles to participate. Men, women and children made this hard voyage; they slept in barns and farm houses along the way and were fed by the settlers' wives.

The annual open-air communion service was the high point of the church year in the Highland Presbyterian churches. It was a lengthy ritual, lasting for five days[19] that began on a Thursday with fasting and preparation. Friday's service was devoted to discussion of a religious question proposed by a prominent member of the congregation. To consider this question, an elder presented a text, and a parishioner responded. The respondents' reply to the text often exhibited a profound knowledge of the scriptures that might be considered remarkable considering their lack of formal education. Saturday was a day of preparation for communion involving two discourses, one in Gaelic, another in English. The Sunday service was the highlight of the communion week. It began at 10:30 in the morning and continued until six in the evening. Devotions began with psalms and prayers and then the minister delivered a sermon addressed to the central truths of redemption. The reception of communion followed. The minister ended the devotions for that day by exhorting the faithful to continue on the path of morality and spirituality. The communion services were followed on Monday by a final service of thanksgiving. This format for the communion service lasted until late in the 19th century, with some open-air services surviving to almost the mid-20th century.

The crowds for these annual communion services were so large that the service had to be held out doors. Church gatherings of all kinds provided a social as well as a spiritual outlet for the people and provided opportunity for fringe festivities involving youthful capers, courting and drinking.[20]

Even before the suffragette movement of the 1890s, which promoted the equality of women in various spheres of life, the Presbyterian church had become aware of the potential contribution of women.[21] Originally this contribution was limited to domestic activities,[22] but as choirs came into vogue in the 1850s and, though rarely, organ music in the 1870s, women began to play an active role in the musical part of the liturgy. Women with good voices sang in the choir, and those with instrumental talent played the organ.

The Missionary Society was the largest organization of Canadian women in the 19th century, and through membership in this society, Canadian women became a significant force in the Presbyterian church.[23] In the late 1800s and early 1900s, auxiliaries of the Missionary Society in Cape Breton numbered in the forties.[24] The prevalence of Gaelic among their members was reflected in the custom of having a chapter from the Scriptures read in Gaelic at their meetings. The work of the Missionary Society reflected the emphasis of the Presbyterian church on evangelism. Women organized missionary societies to study the work of missionaries and to support their endeavours. These societies raised between one-fourth and one-third of the money for the foreign missionary work of the Canadian Presbyterian Church,[25] enabling the organization to carry on its work abroad more effectively. Some Cape Breton members of the Missionary Society went overseas as missionaries.[26] Maude MacKinnon was the first missionary from Sydney. In 1914, she travelled to Korea and later to Manchuria.[27]

Tony MacKenzie of Kenzieville claims that "it was the issue of temperance that got the women of eastern Nova Scotia interested in politics."The Women's Christian Temperance Association, formed in 1883, was closely allied with the Presbyterian church and sought to attain a "Protestant Christian Society." Its fight for prohibition was viewed to be a religious battle.[28] Suffrage was seen as the means for women to gain the political power needed to bring about prohibition and the suffrage movement of Nova Scotia and Canada was closely associated with this goal. Because of the political and social aspirations of the Women's Christian Temperance Association, its members, many of whom were Highland Scots, came to be viewed as reformers. Despite strong opposition, they kept the question of the vote for women before the public.

While some viewed these women as extremists, their aspirations were to reduce the drinking problems affecting many families in the communities of eastern Nova Scotia and Cape Breton. The first settlers reportedly drank very little liquor, but this situation changed in the early 1800s when, as prosperity increased and communities grew, excessive drinking became a problem. Reverend George Patterson gave this account of the worst excesses of drinking in Pictou County in the early decades of the 1800s:

> In [even] the most moral settlements every third or fourth family would have a puncheon of rum, for the supply of themselves and neighbors. In some instances, where there were a number of sons in a family approaching manhood, the whole might be consumed with very little assistance from others. In one large settlement, it was calculated on one occasion, that it had been introduced in the fall at the rate of half a puncheon for each family, and before spring the supply of the same was exhausted. I have heard of a tradesman at his bench taking his glass regularly every hour. A person who worked in a shipyard told me that the allowance to each workman from the employer was three glasses a day, while he was confident that on an average each man drank as many more. A member of my congregation told me of himself and others working at a job for ten days or a fortnight in the heat of summer drinking each their quart bottle of rum a day.[29]

The drinking problem in Pictou County prompted a group of Presbyterian women to organize a branch of the Women's Christian Temperance Union in New Glasgow in 1890. Some of the more zealous members of this branch walked into rum sellers' establishments to try to convince the patrons to give up their enterprise.

Some of these women were reported to have "knelt in prayer in the presence of drunken men and to have besought divine mercy on those who sinned by indulgence in liquor."[30]

While women continued to pursue the causes of evangelism and prohibition, they broadened their contribution to the church in the 20th century by raising funds for building and furnishing their churches, work that continues to this day. Mabel Murray of Westville recalled the work the women of that community put into sponsoring teas for this purpose. "In their own homes they prepared a variety of delicate sandwiches and delicious sweets. Then they brought this food to the church hall where they arranged it attractively on tables set for this purpose. The last thing they did was to prepare and serve tea." They also largely took over responsibility for Sunday school where they taught the basics of Christianity through the study of the Bible and the *Short Catechism*.

The religious fervour of the Presbyterians endured unabated until World War I. Later, in 1925, the Presbyterian Church in Pictou County was rocked by the departure of an estimated one-third to one-half of its members to the newly formed United Church of Canada.[31] This defection deeply divided many Presbyterian families. Agnes Johnston of Thorburn expressed regret regarding "the conflict the coming of the United Church caused within and between families." For the faithful, it was heart-breaking to see their relatives and friends leave the fold—those who left felt that there was a better fit between their more secular world view and the teachings of the United Church.

Roman Catholics

Roman Catholic Scots were most heavily concentrated in Antigonish County on the mainland and in Inverness county in Cape Breton. Their faithful adherence to Catholicism can be partially attributed to the religious oppression to which they were subjected in their native land. Suffering for the cause of their faith seemed to deepen their appreciation of it.

The first large contingent of Catholic Highlanders arrived on the *Dunkheld* in 1791, and other boatloads of Catholics soon followed. In 1801, Catholics arrived on the *Sarah,* the *Dove,* the *Good Intent,* the *Nora* and the *Alexander.*[32] These passengers were also grateful for the hospitality extended by the pioneers of Pictou. Fr.

Angus MacEachern, who had come to Prince Edward Island in 1790 to serve the Highland congregation in that province, crossed over to Pictou to meet the passengers and he encouraged them to move east along the Gulf shore to Lismore and Antigonish; a small number went to Cape Breton. They travelled to their new homes by canoe and settled along the shoreline. After the good land was taken in Antigonish, the Highland Catholics settled in Cape Breton, continuing to arrive, until by 1861 there were 33,326 there.[33] Between 1791 and 1820, Antigonish received the largest number of Catholic immigrants.[34]

The first Highland Catholic parish in eastern Nova Scotia was St. Margaret's at Arisaig.[35] In 1792, the parishioners built the first church, a simple log structure, and Fr. James MacDonald served as the first parish priest there from 1792 to 1797. Following the establishment of that parish, it was reported that three Highland women walked annually from Parrsboro to Arisag, a distance of 150 miles, to make their Easter duty. One of these women, Mary MacLeod, carried her infant grandson in her arms to be baptized at Arisag. This lad grew up to become the first North American-born priest in what is now the Diocese of Antigonish. Among her descendants were one bishop, twenty priests, two religious brothers and eighteen sisters.[36]

Father MacDonald's health was compromised by the hardship of his mission and, by 1797, he was unable to continue serving his parishioners.[37] In the spring of 1798, Bishop MacEachern took over Fr. MacDonald's missionary duties until Fr. Alexander MacDonald was appointed the second pastor of Arisag in 1802. Between 1802 and 1806, his mission extended from Merigomish to Margaree Harbour, including the communities of Margaree, Broad Cove, Justico, Judique and Mabou.[38] When the priest visited these communities, the people came from the surrounding countryside on foot, riding double on horseback, or along the shore by canoe. They assembled for masses, for marriages, for baptisms of infants and for funeral services. By 1823, there were eight Roman Catholic churches in Cape Breton, and the Highland settlements of Margaree, Judique, East Bay and Grand Narrows each had a resident priest.[39] Before and after services the people socialized, engaging in lively conversations and exchanging news and gossip.

Until 1817, the Roman Catholic parishes and missions in Nova Scotia and Cape Breton came under the jurisdiction of the Diocese of Quebec.[40] Bishop Joseph Plessis of Quebec visited parishes and missions in eastern Nova Scotia in 1811, 1812 and 1815. In 1812, he visited parts of Cape Breton, Antigonish and Pictou, and his diaries contain some of his impressions of his congregations in eastern Nova Scotia.[41] On his visit to Port Hood in 1812, he noted that he found himself faced with a population that spoke only Gaelic. He performed his services in a make-shift chapel where he had to compete with the noise of a multitude of dogs and the "babbling and bawling" of a large number of infants. Even though he was somewhat alarmed by the lack of decorum at this and other gatherings of his Highland flock, he had to admit his amazement at the faith of the settlers. He wrote: "The faith of the people ... is so strong that it surpasses all imagination."[42]

From the very beginning of his tenure as Bishop of Quebec, Bishop Plessis made efforts to have his diocese divided into smaller ecclesiastical missions. In 1817, these efforts resulted in the separation of the mainland of Nova Scotia from the Diocese of Quebec, and Nova Scotia was administered by Bishop William Fraser who served as its apostolic vicar.[43] Cape Breton was placed under the jurisdiction of Bishop Angus MacEachern from 1821 to 1827.[44] By 1825, eleven parishes had been organized in eastern Nova Scotia. In 1842, the vicariate of Nova Scotia was changed into the Diocese of Halifax, with Bishop William Fraser as its first head.[45] Finding this jurisdiction also to be too large, Bishop Fraser petitioned Rome to divide Nova Scotia into two dioceses, one to consist of the county of Antigonish and the island of Cape Breton, and the other to include the rest of the province.[46] In 1844, a decree divided Nova Scotia as he had suggested, and the first seat of the eastern Diocese was located at Arichat, with Bishop William Fraser at its head.

When Bishop Fraser died in 1851, Fr. Colin F. MacKinnon became the second bishop of Arichat. Bishop MacKinnon's greatest achievements were in the area of education.[47] He aspired to make a high school education available to young Catholic women, and in 1856 he established the Arichat Convent run by the Sisters of Notre Dame. He was also responsible for establishing St. Francis Xavier College in 1853 in Arichat, the predecessor of St. Francis Xavier University in Antigonish. In 1866, he undertook the monumental task of building the church which stands to this day as St. Ninian's Cathedral in Antigonish. In 1877, Bishop John Cameron became the third bishop of Arichat, and he moved the seat of the diocese and St. Francis Xavier College to Antigonish.[48]

The basic features that distinguished the Roman Catholic church from the Presbyterian church were recognition of the authority of the pope and the centrality of the celebration of mass to Catholic religious services. The celebratory highlights of the Church calendar year were the birth of Christ at Christmas and the resurrection of Christ at Easter. In preparation for these events, the people fasted rigorously and abstained from eating meat during Advent and Lent, the seasons leading up to these celebrations.

The celebration of mass was so important to faithful Catholics that they went to unusual lengths to attend. It was quite common to walk distances of five to fifteen miles to participate in the service. Peggy MacIsaac, St. Andrews, remembers stories her mother told of "female settlers walking this distance barefoot along footpaths through the woods." It is remarkable that they walked these distances while fasting, which meant abstaining from food and water after midnight.

In almost every home, the rosary was recited daily led by either the father or the mother, often in Gaelic, usually followed by one or more litanies. Speaking of her mother, Sr. Sarah MacPherson said, "I will never forget the fervour with which she intoned the litanies following the rosary."

Fig. 11 Official opening of St. Ninian's Cathedral, Antigonish, in 1878. Courtesy Antigonish Heritage Museum. 01.22.

61

Some Highland women attributed the popularity of the rosary to its use as a religious exercise in the home in the days before the settlers had churches in their communities or when they were unable to attend church. Children usually learned their prayers at their mothers' knees as they prayed with them twice daily and as they knelt and recited the rosary with their families. Other common religious rituals in the home were blessings with holy water, lighting blessed candles in time of distress and blessings before and after meals.

Children learned the basic precepts of their faith formally through instruction in school. Bishop Cameron had a Gaelic catechism printed for use in teaching religion to the Highland Scots, and elderly Highland Scottish women interviewed recalled learning their catechism from this book. In most homes there was some reinforcement of the teachings of the catechism through mothers questioning their children about the teachings of the church.

Mothers took prime responsibility for teaching morals to their children, mainly through example, but also by making explicit the high expectations of their children's behaviour. They made clear what they considered right and wrong, and disapproved of any inappropriate behaviour. Jean MacPherson, of St. Andrews, Antigonish County, recalls an early lesson in honesty:

> When I was a little girl, I found a penny in the pew in church which I took home to show to my grandmother. When my grandmother found out where I got the penny, she immediately took me by the hand, walked me back to the church, and made me deposit the penny in the pew from which I took it. This was a lesson in honesty that I never forgot.

There were also many mothers who did not articulate their expectations regarding their children's behaviour, but modelled expected behaviour by their example. Sr. Alexia Cameron of the Sisters of St. Martha put it this way: "Their way of life taught values. We were influenced by the way they lived and prayed." Many descendants of the Highland settlers who are alive today agree that their mothers' examples were the best teachers. Maureen MacGillivray of Antigonish recalled that "women set the moral tone not only in the home but also in the community." This point is echoed by Fr. John Cameron, bishop of the Diocese of Antigonish from 1870 to 1910: "As a rule women had retained a keener sense of Catholic faith and morality than ... the other sex. I honor her ... and depend on her ... to preserve and diffuse Christian morality in the family, and if in the family, then in the state."[49]

Women played a number of supportive, though traditionally female, roles in the church.[50] They took responsibility for cleaning the churches until the parishes could afford janitors. They also looked after cleaning and ironing the priests' vestments on a weekly basis. Many women were active in the Catholic Women's League, which raised money for charitable causes, visited the sick and delivered help to the poor. During the Second World War, they worked with the Red Cross in making quilts and knitted goods to be sent overseas. They also sent greeting cards, candy and cigarettes to young men from the local communities who were serving overseas. Catholic women who joined religious congregations became the arm of the church in carrying out its educational, social and charitable works.

Impact of Religion

Many descendants of the Highland settlers who were interviewed agree that one of the most memorable characteristics of their mothers and grandmothers was their deep and abiding faith. Their sense of spirituality led them to value their faith above all else and to hope that a son or daughter would enter a religious order. "It was a badge of distinction to have a priest in the family," said Jean MacPherson. Presbyterian mothers were equally proud of their sons who entered the ministry. Having a son enter the priesthood or the ministry was a source of prestige for the family, because clerics not only provided spiritual guidance, they also were leaders in the community. In many rural communities, the minister or priest was often the only well-educated person, and people went to him for counsel on moral, spiritual and personal concerns, and even business matters.

The influence of the clergy could extend into the realm of politics; the life of Bishop John Cameron, parish priest in St. Andrews, Antigonish County, is an example of this. He was an ardent Conservative and a close friend and confidante of Sir John Thompson, who was justice Minister under Sir John A. MacDonald and later prime minister. Bishop Cameron's political views were well known and to this day some of the older members of his parish attribute their loyal support of the Conservative party to the influence of Bishop Cameron on their families.

The faith of the Highland Scottish women may have been the most important factor in determining their outlook on life. Their strong and simple faith was a source of consolation and strength in times of distress. It gave meaning to their lives and brought peace and contentment. The belief in another world eased the harshness of their lives, and they valued spiritual wellbeing over earthly possessions. As one thoughtful observer put it: "They bound their appetites by their necessities, and their happiness consists not in having much but in wanting little."[51]

Five

Women's Domestic Activities

The isolation of the Highland Scots in eastern Nova Scotia and Cape Breton resulted in relatively uniform values. A high regard for the institution of marriage in Scotland carried over to North America. Girls' primary aspirations were to be wives and mothers.[1] It was customary for women to marry in their late teens, and for their husbands to be somewhat older. The family was the center of a married woman's universe, the source of her joys, sorrows, hopes, fears and aspirations, and most women put the needs of their husbands and children before their own. The deep attachment between wife and husband was part of a reciprocal relationship that has its basis in the culture of the Highlands of Scotland. One comment on Highland husbands noted: "It is well known that the Highlanders are remarkably delicate toward their women; and that, in matrimonial life, their fidelity and attachment cannot be surpassed."[2]

This view of the marital relationship is an ideal which marriages approximated to varying degrees. The chief blemish on the reputation of Highland husbands was the widespread use of alcohol, which, when consumed excessively, compromised the well-being of their families. Their use of liquor, which the Highland men lovingly called "the water of life,"[3] had a long and noble tradition as a mark of hospitality, and therefore drinking was a custom that was hard to curb. Excessive drinking made it hard for men to adequately provide for their families, placing an additional burden

Fig. 12 Family scene. Courtesy Hector *Exhibit Centre.*

on their wives and children. In extreme cases, their drinking led to violence, which affected the security of their families.

Even though Highland women viewed themselves to be subordinate to their husbands, there were variations in the power relationship between the two. At one extreme we find excessively tyrannical husbands who expected their wives to be submissive in every area of their relationship. Frances MacIsaac, of Brierly Brook, described these men as tough and demanding: "They used the term 'woman' to address their wives in a domineering fashion when they were giving orders. 'Woman, get my tea.' 'Woman, get my dinner.' 'Woman, get my pipe.' This is the way they talked. Thank God there were not too many of them."

There were some women who, by nature or social circumstances, were submissive. These women are not to be confused with women whose influence was often masked by the quiet and subtle ways in which their influence was exercised. As noted by Maureen MacGillivray, of Antigonish, "The men thought they were in charge, but the women knew how to get around them." At the other extreme, there are reports of domineering women. Highland women's ability to exercise influence has a long tradition and is captured in this view of its origin:

> One of the most notable and easily documentable charac-
> teristics of Celtic tribal society ... is the place in it of tough,
> strong-minded women. This is the hidden world of matriarchy,

exercising power indirectly, which existed over and against the masculine authority of the chief.[4]

Some informants suggested that this hidden matriarchal world remains intact. Complicating the relationship between men and women were their different spheres of influence. Women who were subject to their husbands in their marital relations were known to exercise the greatest influence in decisions regarding the education of their children and at least equal influence in economic decisions affecting their families.

Single Women

Single women from the Highlands and Islands of Scotland accompanied families to Nova Scotia on immigrant ships between 1773 and 1850. They were permitted to take passage if accompanied by a father or a brother, or if they were with a family with whom they had some association.[5] After their arrival in Nova Scotia, they continued to live with the families with whom they came, at least for a while. Most of these women did not remain single for long. Some came because they were engaged to be married to men already in the colony; some married unattached males whom they knew or met on the crossing; others married young men from the communities in which they settled; some women did not marry.

Living as they did in isolated rural communities where there were uniform social standards and few economic opportunities outside the home, single women, and their successors for generations to come, were expected to assume certain roles in the family

Fig. 13 The extended family of a widow: her brother, sister, daughter and grandchild. Courtesy Antigonish Heritage Museum. 96.98.

67

and in the community.[6] Single women often stepped in to help their mothers in household duties or to care for children if a family member died. Single female relatives also performed the household duties for mothers who were ill or confined by child birth. Betty Ballantyne of Cape George paid tribute to the generosity of those single women "who sacrificed their own aspirations to stay home and take care of sick parents and relatives." Some single women kept house for single brothers; some served as housekeepers for priests. Single women were often called upon and expected to lend a hand when someone in the community needed help, and they were frequently seen carrying baskets of food through the community to be delivered to people in need. Gradually, single women made their way into the labour force as employment opportunities became available, first in domestic labour and teaching, later in clerical and secretarial work, retail trades and nursing.

Motherhood

Highland women aspired to be the best mothers they could be. While not all women lived up to this ideal, most were devoted to their children and viewed them as gifts from God. Florence MacDougall from Inverness County is typical of this devotion in her statement: "My children are my life." The devotion of these women to their children brought fulfillment to their lives, and children reciprocated with a strong sense of duty to their parents, looking after them through sickness and old age.[7] Filial duty is a communal attribute that was deeply engrained in the Highland Scots.

The Highland Scots of eastern Nova Scotia and Cape Breton usually had large families.[8] It was common for parents to have ten or more children—until the 1950s, a family of six was considered small. This tendency partially reflected the influence of the Catholic church, which taught that women were to be subject to their husbands. In addition, before the coming of technology and medical advancements that reduced infant mortality rates, parents viewed their children as economic assets. More children meant more hands in the home and on the farm. The lot of the mother of a large family was a hard one, but it was made more bearable by being viewed as the will of God.[9]

Fig. 14 A common style of farmhouse in the early 1900s. Courtesy Antigonish Heritage Museum. 2003.053.016.

Fig. 15 Typical country farmhouse in Lochaber. Courtesy Antigonish Heritage

There was usually a midwife available in each community to assist with the delivery of babies. Anna MacDonald of Maryvale pointed out that the midwife's work went beyond medical assistance."After delivering a baby, they often remained in the home for several days in order to take over the housework for the mother." Most mid-wives learned their trade by observing other mid-wives in action. Mid-wives continued this service for some time after hospitals were introduced into eastern Nova Scotia in the early 1900s because these hospitals originally did not have maternity facilities and because people still lived in relative isolation from such institutions. While women tended to rejoice in their children and prize their large families, child-bearing cost some of the less robust among them their lives. Sr. Sarah MacPherson of the Sisters of St. Martha told this story of her grandmother's death:

> She had married at the age of eighteen, had ten children by the
> time she was thirty-two, and the wear and tear of child bearing
> and child rearing led to her early death. Her place in the family
> was taken by her two oldest daughters, aged ten and twelve.
> One of these dear little girls was so small that she had to stand
> on a chair to knead the dough for the daily bread.

The families of the original Highland settlers and several generations of their descendants were economically self-sufficient, if relatively poor.[10] Home and work were not separate. The domestic activities of women included a great deal of productive work, which gave them a major economic role in the family. The majority of these women were vigorous and hardy, and they did all the housework and a good deal of the work outside of the house, including many of the on-going activities associated with farming. In this work they were often assisted by their children and by members of their extended families. Instead of being economically dependent on their husbands, they were partners in the productive work of the homestead, and alongside their husbands they produced the goods necessary for subsistence. While their lives were hard, they were also challenging and rewarding.

Highland families were usually extended families; in most homes there were several adult female relatives—a grandmother, a single aunt or a sister—who, if in good health, shared the work of the household. They also took over the work of wives who were sick or frail. Men were preoccupied with heavy outside work, such as clearing the land, breaking ground and procuring wood for the fire. In this work they were often assisted by male members of the extended family.

Highland women had the reputation of being better workers than Highland men, a view of female labour that originated in the Highlands and carried over into North America. In the clan system, men devoted themselves to serving the chief, while women stayed home and did the housework and much of the farm work.

While men worked at clearing the forests and fields or sometimes pursued paid work on road construction, women continued to do a significant amount of work on the farm, regardless of their household duties. In the spring they helped with the planting by digging and hoeing the ground and by sowing seeds. In the fall they helped with harvesting the crop and bringing in the vegetables for winter storage. Their barn work entailed feeding the livestock

Fig. 16 Farm chores. Courtesy Hector *Exhibit Centre.*

and milking the cows. Over time, the men took over the majority of these chores, a change that coincided with the development of technology to assist with these tasks. As early as the 1850s, some farm implements, including the plough, the harrow, the cultivator, the drill harrow, the sowing machine and the roller, were adver-

Fig. 17 c.1950. Courtesy MacDonald House Museum.   *Fig. 18 Courtesy* Hector *Exhibit Centre.*

tised for sale, but many farmers did not have sufficient income in cash or in kind to afford them.[11] In the early 1880s, the mowing machine and the horse rake were added to the list of available farm implements,[12] but several decades passed before these machines replaced the scythe and the hand rake.

Housework

The spartan facilities of the original pioneer dwellings made their upkeep a challenge. In log cabins with earthen floors and beds made of straw or spruce boughs, maintaining cleanliness was difficult. Because of the limited supply of clothing, a change of clothing was

71

Fig. 19 Sawing wood. Courtesy Antigonish Heritage Museum. 2003.053.026.

infrequent, and while this made for a limited amount of wash, the chore of washing these clothes by hand was heavy. Equally heavy was the work involved in lugging water from the brook, chopping firewood and kindling, carrying them into the house and feeding the greedy fire in the fireplace or later the woodstove.

The wives' domestic chores of cleaning and washing changed as people built frame houses with wooden floors and acquired a supply of bedding and clothing. The wooden floors required sweeping and scrubbing, and older women recalled how their mothers used to spread sand on the softwood floors and rub it in with a scrub brush to make the floors look like new. As the supply of bedding and clothing became greater, the amount of washing increased accordingly. Pioneer women did this backbreaking work without the benefit of running water and washing machines. Many of their descendants have memories of the heavy labour involved in carrying endless buckets of water from a well or spring in winter to do a wash. When the weather permitted, the women often took their wash to a brook where they scrubbed the clothes on a washboard, using a cake of homemade soap. Combining washday with a picnic helped to reduce the drudgery of the work. Christena MacDonald of Pleasant Valley described wash day at the brook:

> We spent the whole day at the brook with my mother, and we combined the chore of washing with a picnic. We started the job by gathering a bunch of stones on which to start a fire. After the fire was started, we hauled water out of the brook and put it in an iron boiler over the fire. When the water was hot, we put the fire out, and Mother used a washboard and a cake of

home-made soap to scrub the dirt out of the clothes. As she finished washing each piece of clothing, we took it from her, and we rinsed it in the brook. When we got tired, Mother would announce it was time for a rest and would bring out a picnic basket; then we would sit and relax by the brook, sometimes with our feet dangling in the water, and we would enjoy our food. When we finished our break, we went back to work to finish the wash and hang it on the bushes to dry. Some of the heavier clothes were laid on rocks on the bank of the river. While the clothes were drying, we would go for a swim and then stretch out on the grass beside the brook. This mixture of work and pleasure made us look forward to wash day.

Hand-cranked washing machines were in use in some rural homes in the 1930s, before the coming of electric washing machines. Many Highland women were fastidious about the cleanliness of their houses, clothes and linens, and Irene MacDonald from East Bay noted that the reputation of female members of their community depended on it. "Married women were judged by the houses they kept. Being a good housekeeper was a source of prestige in the community."

Food Preparation

Oral testimony provides a great deal of information about food production, gathering and preparation.[13] The diet of the pioneers consisted primarily of potatoes and dishes made from oats and wheat, supplemented by game and fish from forest and stream. Using only crude cooking utensils, women prepared the simple foods that were the staples of the pioneer diet, sometimes turning them into culinary delights. C. I. N. MacLeod's story about the *bannock* of ashes illustrates this point:

A traveler newly arrived from Scotland was alarmed when he saw the woman of the house where he was a guest place the unbaked bannock in the smouldering embers, place powdered ashes around it and burning embers over it. When she knew the bannock was cooked, she took it out of the embers, and she dusted off the ashes with a bleached linen cloth. The guest admitted that no morsel of bread ever tasted so good.[14]

Over time, food preparation became more sophisticated. When the immigrants had cleared several acres of land, the variety of vegetables they grew was enlarged to include turnips, carrots, parsnips, onions, beets and cabbage, in addition to the original staple, potatoes. As they continued to clear land, the quantity and variety of vegetables increased further, and the women became proficient in pickling, bottling, preserving and canning. Many frame houses had root cellars in which the settlers stored vegetables throughout the winter.

Strawberries, raspberries, blueberries, blackberries, gooseberries and cranberries grew wild in great quantities in the surrounding fields. The choppings left from felling the trees proved to be particularly fertile ground for producing bumper crops of raspberries and blackberries. Women who grew up in Brown's Mountain in Antigonish County reported that whole families would go by horse and wagon to a good berry patch, bring large containers for the berries and a good picnic lunch and they would spend a whole day picking berries. They returned with buckets and baskets of berries, which were not only eaten fresh, but also turned into delicious preserves, jellies and pies. Wild apples added to the variety of fruits available and they became a versatile product. Apples were stewed, baked, jellied and used as filling in pies. Many homes had cold kitchens and pantries which enabled people to keep baked goods for several days and preserves for the winter months.

Fig. 20 Building the trunk road over Brown's Mountain to the interior of Antigonish in 1873. Courtesy Antigonish Heritage Museum. 99.136.3

After a number of years of successful efforts to remove the stumps from the fields, families cleared sufficient acreage to support livestock, such as pigs, sheep, cows and horses. A booklet published in 1843 to provide information for settlers advised women that they were expected to be dairy-maids.[15] And that they were. It was a Highland tradition that no self-respecting man would be seen milking a cow. Florence MacDougall from Inverness County laughed as she told the story of her brother who was persuaded to learn how to milk. "I remember one day he saw someone coming as he was milking, and he was so embarrassed that he threw the milk bucket on the ground and ran." Descendants of the settlers claim that many cows would not let down their milk until a woman sang to them, a myth probably designed to keep women doing the milking. Early farms had only a few cows. In 1899, a report from the Nova Scotia Department of Agriculture expressed regret that the farmers were not increasing the number of cows to produce the milk needed to keep the creameries supplied.[16] The situation did not change quickly. Statistics for Antigonish County for 1921

Fig. 21 Women feeding calves. Courtesy Antigonish Heritage Museum. 91.400.001.

Fig. 22 Preparing to milk the cows. Courtesy Antigonish Heritage Museum. 2004.068.001.

75

revealed that the number of cows per farm reached a high of four in 1921 only to decline again to 3.1 per farm in 1931.[17] The size of the dairy herds did not increase substantially until the 1940s.

The cows were prized for their milk and their meat. Milk produced cream, butter, cheese, curds, buttermilk and *fuarag*, a mixture of cream and rolled oats. Homemade butter and cheese were the major products of the rural home and were used as a medium of exchange. Buttermilk was a by-product of the churning process. Curds and cheese were made by removing the solids from the milk. These products added both nutrition and variety to the diet. Milk and cream were placed in large containers and lowered into wells to be kept cold. Before the advent of the cream separator, women would let the milk stand until the cream rose to the top and then skim it to be churned into butter. Cream separators were available for purchase by the late 1800s and early 1900s, but because most farm people did not have the money to buy them, few were in use.[18]

Every family tried to have a steer, a lamb, and a pig ready for butchering in the fall. The women made sure that every bit of the carcass of each animal was used. Josephine MacIsaac from Antigonish recalls how her uncles and her grandmother used every part of the animal in the 1930s and 1940s:

> Before the men put the steer down, Grandma brought a bucket to the barn to collect the blood that was to be drawn from the animal. This blood was brought into the kitchen where it was cooked with suet, oatmeal and spices to make tasty blood puddings. The men carefully skinned the animal so that its hide could be set aside to be made into leather. From the head of the animal they removed the tongue and the meat. Grandma put a pot of water on the stove in which to boil the tongue. Tongue was considered to be a delicacy. She chopped the meat from the head of the steer and combined it with chopped meat from the head of a pig to make potted head. The lining of the stomach, the intestines, the kidneys and the liver were all put to good use. When the men completed the butchering, they took the lining of the stomach and the intestines to the brook to clean them in the fresh, cold water. The cleaned intestines served as casings for the blood puddings. The men washed and scraped the lining of the stomach and then took it back to the kitchen to be cut into small pieces and later fried in butter. This dish was known as tripe. The men sliced the liver to be fried with pork and onions.

The kidneys were chopped up to be used with other meats in making *isbean*. After the carcass of the animal was cooled and aged for several days, the men cut it into roasts, steaks, stew meat and soup bones. Some of this meat was eaten fresh. Some of it was salted for the winter. When the men were cutting up the carcass, they removed the tallow from the meat. Grandma rendered the tallow for use as a fat in frying and in baking and as the main ingredient in making soap. Not even the tail of the animal went to waste. Grandma boiled it with vegetables to make soup. All of this activity took several or more days and turned my grandmother's kitchen into a small manufacturing plant.

Families enjoyed the luxury of a supply of fresh meat for weeks after the animals were butchered. With sleds hauled by horses, farmers were able to go to the lakes in winter to cut large squares of ice to be used for the preservation of meat and fish. These squares of ice were stored in ice-houses.[19] Meat and fish were inserted between cakes of ice, and the cakes of ice were then surrounded by sawdust for insulation. This method of preservation kept meat and fish frozen for months.

Advertisements for cooking stoves appeared in the Antigonish *Casket* in the late 1850s. The women reacted with delight to the replacement of the fireplace by the cast-iron, wood-burning kitchen stove which provided facilities for cooking, baking and heating.

Fig. 23 Feeding orphaned lambs. Courtesy Antigonish Heritage Museum. 95.250.4.

77

While food was cooking on the stove, the men often sat with their sock feet on the oven door to enjoy the warmth of the wood stove and the smell of the good food. To this day many old folks claim that there is nothing like the smell and heat of a wood-burning fire. They have fond memories of the comforts the wood stove and the food produced on it provided. Sr. Mairi Macdonald, a historian of Highland Scottish descent from Inverness County, celebrated the sensual delights of the food prepared in the old country kitchen:

> The kitchen stove ... is a source of delectable odours. The busy women ... draw from their ovens such mouth-watering things as currant loaf soon to be dripping with nutty country butter, big sour-cream biscuits waiting for the delicate tartness of gooseberry jam, carroway cookies lightly dusted with sugar and—that most pervasive childhood memory—the crusty, fluffy, homemade bread. Climaxing the achievement of the old farm kitchen were black and white puddings (*maragan*), a sausage (*isbean*) and haggis.... Familiar delicacies were the tangy country cheese, and the thick yellow cream rising on the pans set to cool on high shelves. You just picked up a corner of this cream with a big spoon and lifted the whole top off. Then you were on your way to the incomparable mixture of oatmeal and cream (*fuarag*) or the crimson and gold mash of strawberries and cream.[20]

She concluded with the assessment that "when one considers what our modern age has brought us in powdered, canned and packaged food, our Nova Scotian forebears had food fit for gods."[21]

Beginning in the second half of the 19th century, women bartered eggs, butter and cream for food items not produced on the farm. The primary groceries that were available in the early grocery stores were tea, flour, oatmeal, rolled oats, sugar, molasses, dry fish and herring. Canned goods began to be advertised for sale as early as 1890.[22] In lieu of bartering, some women sold eggs, cream and butter for cash.[23] Descendants of the immigrants agreed that it was understood in the family that this money belonged to the wife to be used as she saw fit, even when her husband took the goods to market for her. With this cash, women purchased items for the home such as curtains, sheets, towels, dishes and flatware from local dry-goods stores and from the Eaton's catalogue. Some bartering continued right up until World War II. The farm women made all of the butter that was used in urban areas until creameries were established around the turn of the century.

Women who bartered or sold farm produce were particularly hard hit during the Depression of the 1930s when they were less able to find a market for their products. Because the money they got from selling farm goods was the only source of cash for many farm families, these families often found themselves short of money when they needed to pay their property taxes. Money was so scarce at this time that some farmers had no choice but to sell a cow to raise the money for their taxes. On an average farm, where there were usually only three or four cows, the loss of even one could prove to be a great hardship.

Fig. 24 Ready for market, c.1930s. Courtesy St. FX Archives. 89-1250.

Until the 1940s, women used folk remedies, many from the Scottish Highlands, to treat most illnesses.[24] They gathered herbs and roots to boil for medicinal purposes. The women also took measures to guard against illness by giving family members a dose of sulphur and molasses in the spring to clean out the system. Children were administered a daily dose of cod liver oil to ward off colds and other contagious illnesses.

Clothing

Like the food, the clothing too was produced in the home.[25] This task involved the joint effort of all the women of the household. Annie MacDonald from Lismore remembers how in the old days the production of clothing kept all the women busy:

> When the men had sheared the sheep, the mother, with the aid of her sister and her daughters, washed, combed and carded the wool, and spun it into yarn. Then the wool was ready for knitting or weaving. I remember how the old women sat beside

79

the stove and spent most of the day knitting socks, stockings, underwear, *mocans* [a form of footwear made out of wool] mitts, sweaters and coats. Then the attention of the women turned to weaving. On their hand looms they wove the wool into cloth. Some of them developed great skill in making dyes from moss, berries and leaves to provide color to make the cloth look more attractive. Out of the woven cloth they made homespun pants and shirts and coats for the men and boys and homespun blouses and skirts or dresses for the women and girls. Ah, I am old enough to remember the homespuns. I can even remember when I wore them.

After clothes became available in stores, some Highland Scots were embarrassed to wear homespuns, but others concurred with Jenny MacQuarrie's view that "well-made homespuns looked just as good as store-bought clothing." Differences in the quality of the home-made clothes could be attributed to variations in the skills and artistry of the maker.

Fig. 25 Knitting, c.1920. Courtesy MacDonald House Museum.

Fig. 26 Spinning, c.1900. Courtesy MacDonald House Museum.

So much effort went into preparing cloth and yarn that women made sure that none of it was wasted. Bits of surplus cloth and yarn were saved to be turned into braided or hooked mats or rugs as well as quilts. The artistry with which the best of these products was crafted made them works of art. Evening was the time when the women did the sewing, the knitting and the hooking. They often sat near the fire and sang while they made clothes, bedding or floor coverings. Sometimes their husbands sat with them and joined in the singing.

Fig. 27 A spinning frolic in Antigonish County. Courtesy Antigonish Heritage Museum. 98.47.

Weaving gave rise to the social event known as the milling frolic. When large bolts of cloth were prepared, a milling frolic was held to full or soften the course cloth and to give it a nap.[26] Neighbours came together to turn this activity into an enjoyable social event, and they worked to the rhythm of songs composed for the work. In addition to the singing, there were conversations, food and forms of merriment such as fiddling and dancing. The women also used frolics to socialize while preparing clothing and bedding. They held knitting, quilting, spinning and hooking frolics,[27] and the lively conversations and songs that accompanied the work provided women with a social network and solidarity that offset the isolation of rural life. They were there for one another, and this support carried them through a great deal of adversity.

The men too used the frolic to assist with the heavy work on the farm or in the woods. In each rural community the men went from house to house cutting wood, ploughing, mowing, reaping and threshing.[28] Men's frolics entailed work for women too, for it required them to prepare meals for the hungry workers. Anna MacDonald of Maryvale noted that "the women in one house often tried to outdo the women in other houses in the community in the quality of the meals they prepared. The men looked forward to these fine meals." The day frolic was often followed by a night frolic devoted to dancing to the music of the fiddle.

81

Sometimes, women were relieved of some of the work involved in making clothes. Skilled artisans came to Nova Scotia during and after the Clearances and most communities had an itinerant tailor who would go to a home and prepare a suit and other garments for the man of the house. The tailor remained in the home until the garments were completed, and for his services he received cash and board. A son of a pioneer, Angus MacQuarrie of Arisag, suggested that "none of the suits available in the local stores could match the fine quality of the suits prepared by the best tailors from the cloth of the loom." Like the tailors, shoemakers too went from home to home to prepare footwear for the entire family.

In the 1870s, preparation of cloth and yarn began to move outside the home with the establishment of mills with carding machines, spinning jacks, power looms, dye works, fulling and pressing machines which used steam and water power. In 1871, one of these mills advertised cloth and yarn for cash, or in exchange for wool or other produce.[29] Adding wool to the goods used for barter or cash enabled women to avail themselves of this service. Many of them saved a great deal of labour by exchanging tub-washed wool for cloth.

Eventually the artisans opened their own businesses, and this led to centralization of these services in towns in the late 1800s. Antigonish, to a large extent, was a self-contained community.[30] Leather was made in the local tanneries; boots, shoes, harnesses and saddles were made in small shops; wool was processed in local carding and fulling mills, and converted into knitted wear in the home; and cloth was made by local weavers. In 1880, fifty-seven people were employed in tailoring, dress-making and millinery establishments in Antigonish.[31] Women bartered for yard goods and had tailors prepare some of the clothing for the family, particularly suits and coats. But the clothing requirements of most families were so large that a great deal of it continued to be made in the home; few large families could afford to pay a tailor for all their clothing needs.

The preparation of clothing in the home was facilitated by the arrival of the sewing machine. The Singer Sewing Machine Company opened a branch in New Glasgow in 1900,[32] and advertisements for sewing machines began to appear in the local papers. For those who could afford it, this device greatly reduced the labour and time involved in making clothing.

Charles W. Dunn's interviews conducted a half-century ago with older Highland folks, female as well as male, reveal that, in spite of all the hard work they did, the Highlanders "never spoke of their own experience with regret or resentment."[33] Time may have clouded informants' memories of the hardships they faced and heightened the sense of satisfaction they gained from dealing with difficult challenges and overcoming adversity.

Public Utilities and Home Improvement

Public utilities were introduced to the urban areas of eastern Nova Scotia at the end of the 19th century, and rural women watched with interest as these utilities made domestic chores easier for urban women. Lugging water from wells, springs or brooks was eliminated by the installation of public water systems. The town of New Glasgow constructed a reservoir in 1888, and pumped water from the East River.[34] The water works for the town of Antigonish was installed in 1891.[35] Some of the mining towns in Cape Breton installed water systems as early as 1904. With the inauguration of town water systems, people were able to install indoor toilets in areas where there were community cesspools to collect the waste. Cesspools handled the waste until sewers were built, usually following the construction of streets.

In many of the towns and villages in eastern Nova Scotia, electricity was introduced on a small scale at about the same time as public water systems. Electric power was localized and highly unreliable, and the majority of the power plants were small and privately owned.[36] The Sydney Gas and Electric Company was incorporated in 1888 and was the first supplier of electricity in industrial Cape Breton. Pictou County had electricity as early as 1890 when New Glasgow installed a coal-fired steam-generating plant that powered the flickering light bulbs used in commercial shops and affluent homes.[37] Electricity was introduced in Antigonish on a small scale in 1893.[38] By 1934 all incorporated towns and cities in Nova Scotia had some kind of an electrical system.[39] In the early days, the supply of electricity was not sufficient to meet demand, and its usage in most towns had to be rationed. Maureen MacGillivray reported on the early practices associated with the rationing of electricity in the town of Antigonish: "The town designated one day for washing, another day for baking, and specified the hour on which the lights were to be turned off." Full-time, all-night lighting came to some urban areas as early as 1920 and was quite an improvement over kerosene lamps. With the coming of electricity, the chores of cleaning the lamps, filling them with kerosene, lighting them and carrying them from room to room were eliminated.

The first major appliance to make its way into homes after they received electricity was the washing machine, which started to show up in urban homes in the 1920s.[40] Older Highland women recall what a relief it was to dispense with the wash board. The refrigerator that appeared shortly after the washing machine altered shopping and eating habits. In the 1920s, small appliances such as irons, toasters, percolators and grills became available in Nova Scotia, but the demand for them was small.[41] With the exceptions of the refrigerator and the washer, appliances were not bought in great quantities until after World War II. By the 1930s, electric stoves had become competitive with oil, gas and wood-fired kitchen stoves. The move to electric stoves was only possible after people installed furnaces to heat their homes. Rural women reported that when they went to town they marvelled at these appliances and longed for release from their heavy labour.

A few rural communities managed to tap into the power sources of the towns, and the little electricity they obtained was used primarily for lighting. The provincial government viewed the development of electrical power for rural areas to be so vital that rural electrification was addressed by public policy. The provincial government established the Nova Scotia Power Commission in 1919 to regulate power development in Nova Scotia. In 1937, the Nova Scotia government made rural electrification a provincial priority with the enactment of the Rural Electrification Act and establishment of the Department of Rural Electrification to facilitate greater distribution of electricity.[42] The principle purpose of the Act was to make provision for the subsidization of rural lines. There was a call for more public control of electricity, and it was achieved through the take-over of private power companies by the public utility.[43] The introduction of large-scale dairy farming was dependent on rural electrification and electricity served those dwellings along rural roads and in small hamlets. In 1931, 8.3 per cent of the farms in Nova Scotia had electricity; ten years later 26 per cent of Nova Scotia's farms had it.

The construction of rural lines was hampered during World War II by the scarcity of materials and equipment. Difficulties in building electrical lines were encountered in the sparsely populated areas of Nova Scotia, especially along the rocky coastal areas and in the rugged portions of northern Cape Breton. Substantial progress in rural electrification came after the war, but it was not until the early 1950s that the job was completed. On the farm the electric water pump was the "appliance without peer," for it meant water for both the household and the livestock.[44] It provided women with water for washing, cleaning and cooking. Electricity brought rural women a welcome release from the drudgery of many household and farm chores.

Six

Highland Women in Their Nova Scotia Communities

Social welfare in eastern Nova Scotia and Cape Breton communities was originally a family responsibility that was closely related to Highland communal hospitality and culture. "The old Highlanders were so remarkable for their hospitality that their doors were always left open as if to invite the hungry traveller to walk in and partake of their meals."[1] Frequent references to the hospitality for which the Highland women noted are to be found in their obituaries in *The Casket*. One of these obituaries reads, "Her hospitality had that Highland naturalness that had its spring in an innate love of people and a deep and abiding concern for their welfare."[2]

Highland Scots believed that welfare comes from the home and from the heart. Jean MacPherson, of St. Andrews, notes that "families viewed welfare to be a form of charity." Betty Ballantyne, of Cape George, remembers the kindness and generosity of her family. "I saw my mother take the last loaf of bread in the house to someone who needed it more," she said. Families took care of the less fortunate until this service was taken over by the social welfare system. Transients, orphans, the elderly and the poor turned to families for help. The transients to whom families extended kind treatment have been colourfully described as including "peddlers on horseback or on foot, gypsies in their covered wagons, hobos, ne'er-do-wells and old folks having no permanent abode and who depended on charity as they begged their way."[3] The women of the house took these people in and fed and clothed them. Many descendants of the early settlers claim that no one was ever turned away from their doors.[4] This story from Peggy MacIsaac, of Sylvan Valley, illustrates this point:

> My sister and I had just finished thoroughly cleaning the bed-rooms of our house and had washed all the bedclothes when the dirtiest of the peddlers came walking up our driveway. I told him that we had no room for him. As he walked away, our mother, returning from her garden, met him and invited him in and gave him the best bedroom in the house. And she said to us in a stern voice, "You never, ever turn a person away."

Mary Ann Boyd of Lakevale, recalled that her husband, a fisher-man, found an old homeless man on the wharf, brought him home, and together they cared for him until he died. "In the old days," she said, "we looked after everyone." But as the number and size of communities, the number of homeless people increased to the point where families no longer had the resources to look after all of them. The homeless were people who did not have family ties,[5] and they survived by scrounging food and lodging throughout the countryside. Homeless women went from house to house, often doing housework in each for a few weeks to obtain food and shelter in return for their labour. Homeless men went from farm to farm, cutting and chopping wood, ploughing and doing other farm chores for their keep. Anna MacDonald, of Maryvale, stated that "the rural widow with young children was particularly appreciative of the help the homeless provided."

Despite the large number of people associated with the extended family, families managed to take care of homeless children. Orphans were taken in by relatives, and children born out of wedlock were usually raised as part of the extended family of one of their parents. The mentally challenged continued to be looked after by their families throughout their lives, but because of the stigma attached to mental disability, they were often hidden away at home. Common are accounts of such family members seated shyly behind the kitchen stove—part of, but apart from family activities.

The Widow

Until the 1950s, there was little state-supported social welfare; when a husband died, the widow and her family, for the most part, had to fend for themselves. It was a custom in Highland Scottish families for the family farm to pass from the father to the eldest son. The father usually transferred the deed to the land in the later years of his life. "With this transaction went the understanding that the mother would continue to live in the family home and to run it as long as she was able to do so."[6] The son was to take over the farm in order to help his mother and to look after her in her declining years. These obligations to the mother help to account for the number of Highland Scottish males that did not marry and it was quite common for the oldest son to forgo his own educational and career aspirations in order to help his family.

Widows with young children had to be largely self-reliant. In 1930, the Mothers Allowance was introduced for widows with children, but it was granted on the basis of a means test, and even for those who did qualify, the benefits were small.[7] Widows in rural communities with young children made valiant efforts to survive by maintaining their homesteads.[8] In addition to their domestic duties, they took over every aspect of the farm work which they performed with the assistance of their children, relatives and neighbours, who were particularly sensitive to the widows' need for help with heavy chores. Neighbours helped with the plowing and the harrowing in the fall and spring and with the cutting of logs for firewood in the winter. When widows had animals ready for slaughter, the neighbours did the butchering and the meat cutting.

It was also customary for a single female relative of a widow to move in and take over some of the household chores. Mothers who lived with their widowed daughters helped with tasks like knitting, sewing and cooking. Some widows had female relatives working in the United States who helped by sending clothes to be made over for the children.

In the towns and villages, widows tried to obtain gainful employment. Some took in laundry on a regular basis; others went to work doing domestic chores. Extensive building of roads from the early 1900s to the 1920s created a strong demand for boarding houses for road workers all over eastern Nova Scotia, and some widows converted their homes into boarding houses. In fact, keeping boarding houses was an occupation dominated by widows.[9] Some widows moved into town from rural areas to run boarding houses, and to provide a continuous source of fresh food for the boarding house, the widow often planted a vegetable garden and kept a cow, a pig and a few hens. These women are fondly remembered for the good meals they served. Many Highland Scottish widows were reputed never to have turned a hungry person away from their doors. Their compassion toward the less fortunate is captured in these lines from a widow's obituary: "Many were the free meals served at her table. Hers was not the heart to turn the hungry away."[10]

A few widows took advantage of professional, business and clerical opportunities. Widows who were trained to teach often returned to the classroom. Those with an entrepreneurial bent sometimes managed to open their own stores, which were usually dressmaking or millinery establishments or a combination of both. In many small communities widows served as telephone operators or post mistresses with the offices in their homes. At election time, polling booths were usually located in widow's homes to provide them with some extra cash. Fr. R. B. MacDonald from Sydney, a son of a widow, expressed amazement at the ability of widows "to make do."

Public Welfare

In the latter half of the 18th century, the government of Nova Scotia, realizing that not all families had the resources to care for the poor and the infirm, started to share responsibility for poor relief. In Nova Scotia, poor relief was originally modelled on the Elizabethan Poor Law of 1601 according to which public responsibility for relief of the dependent poor was to be financed and administered by the smallest unit of government.[11] In 1763, the government of Nova Scotia passed a Poor Law based on this model. Financial and administrative responsibility for the relief of the poor fell to towns and counties and there were occasional provincial grants in the case of emergencies. Each municipal council was to appoint three overseers of the poor in each district who would provide relief and support to indigents who were residents of their district.[12] The implementation of poor relief progressed slowly in Nova Scotia;

impoverished rural governments awarded financial aid for the establishment of poor houses to the lowest bidder.

The County Incorporation Act of 1879 and the Town Incorporation Act of 1888 placed responsibility for the care of the poor on the municipal units.[13] Between 1885 and 1900 most counties stopped boarding out the poor and established town and county poor houses.[14] The coming of the poor house checked the growth of paupers looking for municipal aid, for they did not want to be identified as candidates for the poor house. Mary MacIsaac, from Beauly, said that the poor preferred to rely on the charity of hospitable families, and they "would do without rather than risk the humiliation of being sent to the poor house."

Until the 1950s, most of the elderly worked as long as their physical and mental health permitted. Before Old Age Pension was introduced, seniors who could no longer work sought a safe haven with some member of their family or other close relative. According to Marie MacDonald from East Bay:

> Old folks had no choice but to fall back on their families. In many homes one could find several old people from the ranks of grandparents, aunts and uncles. Their addition to the number of people already in the household often made for cramped quarters.

In the Highland Scottish family, old age was revered and children felt a deep sense of duty to look after their parents and other senior members of their extended family. This cultural norm also brought grandchildren in close contact with the richness of their culture through their grandparents' tales.

Limited use of the poor house was made by elderly women. Most of them stayed in their homes supported by their children.[15] The stigma attached to being in the poor house was described in these terms:

> The disgrace of ending one's life in the poor house reflected failure, not only in terms of the lack of material success but also in terms of social relations. It signaled that one was financially impoverished, and also that one lacked the family or social relations that would save one from such a demeaning end.[16]

Despite the negative image of the poor house, it did provide permanent care for the unfortunate few who did not have families to care for them. These people were clothed and fed and given medical attention,[17] but the state of the public economy often limited the quality of assistance.

The facilities of the poor house were spartan. They were heated by wood or coal-fired stoves. Most lacked running water and indoor plumbing. For washroom facilities the men used outdoor privies and the women used rough commodes. The residents slept on straw mattresses with blankets, but no sheets. Able-bodied women washed dishes, swept and scrubbed floors, did the laundry and other housework; able-bodied men helped with the work on the farm associated with the poor house. Their labour helped to subsidize the cost of their care.

Some counties combined facilities for the "harmless insane" and the poor. A report on public charities in Nova Scotia in 1889 gives this description of the clientele of these institutions:

> There are ten insane, either idiots or old people, and all very peaceful and quiet, except one man who has to be locked up.... The others have the run of the house and mingle together freely, old and young, male and female, insane and paupers, without any restraint, and seem to be very contented and happy.[18]

In 1886, the province of Nova Scotia introduced another measure to help the less fortunate by passing legislation that authorized counties to build insane asylums to provide custodial care for the "harmless insane."[19] The differentiation of the care of the "harmless insane" from that of the poor was made on the assumption that the care sufficient for paupers was not suitable for the insane. By 1900, every Nova Scotia county but one had its own asylum, or had arrangements with another county's asylum to receive its "harmless insane," epileptics and "idiots." This measure enabled the province to have the "harmless insane" removed from hospitals. The population of some municipal units, like Antigonish, was not large enough to provide separate institutions for the care of the poor and the "harmless insane."

The population of Pictou County, on the other hand, was large enough to warrant separate institutions.[20] Inverness had a separate county asylum, which was able to survive by receiving clients from the surrounding counties of Richmond and Victoria. Starting in the 1950s, provincial public assistance legislation made alternative provisions for the care of the less fortunate who historically occupied the county homes and asylums. The end of these institutions was long overdue. Their deterioration as well as the government's attitude toward its responsibility for them is reflected in this comment from the Deputy Minister of Public Welfare for Nova Scotia after a fire burned the county home in Antigonish in 1947: "The fire was a good thing, because all the lice, fleas, rats and bedbugs in Antigonish County would have been consumed by it."[21]

Over time, the federal and provincial governments took additional measures to help the poor and the unfortunate outside of institutions. At the turn of the century, the only legal provision for helping these people was the Poor Relief Act.[22] This began to change in the late 1920s and early 1930s as more people questioned laissez-faire ideology as a basis for public social policy. Assistance for the elderly poor who were not institutionalized began with the Federal Old Age Pension Act of 1927,[23] which granted pensions to individuals seventy years of age and older on the basis of a means test. While the amount of money the pension granted eligible seniors was small, its importance is not to be underestimated. Seniors recall with appreciation what receiving the Old Age Pension meant to poor elderly women who had never before received a paycheque. The Old Age Pension became universal with the passage of the Old Age Security Act in 1952 which made provision for a flat-rate benefit for all Canadians who were seventy years of age or older.[24]

The Mothers Allowance was introduced by the Nova Scotia Government in 1930 to help needy widows with two or more children. It was administered on a poor relief or charitable grant basis.[25] The legislation that made provision for this benefit was an important step in the evolution of social welfare because it marked the first acknowledgment by the provincial government of its responsibility toward needy residents.[26] In 1945, the federal government implemented the provisions of the Family Allowance Act which granted a universal family allowance for children under sixteen years of age.[27] These provisions for seniors, widowed mothers and children helped to defray some of the costs extended families bore to provide for the welfare of their members. In the province of Nova Scotia, in 1944, the growing importance of social welfare was recognized by the establishment of a Department of Public Welfare.

Women's Contribution to Community Improvement

In the first half of the 20th century, Highland Scottish women made a contribution to social welfare by participating in voluntary organizations devoted to community improvement. Starting in the 1920s, rural women helped improve their communities through the educational and social programs of the Women's Institute, a Department of Agriculture organization. With headquarters in Truro, the central office assisted local institutes in preparing their programs, providing material for study and, on occasion, providing speakers and demonstrations. Members of the local institutes, with the assistance of the central office, defined the scope of their activities that revolved largely around home, school and community. A summary of the reports for 1929 provides insight into the range of activities performed by this organization.[28] Activities included maintaining a library, providing playground equipment for schools, carrying on regular community work, hospital work, charitable work, arranging public health clinics, assisting school exhibits and assisting with county fairs. The Women's Institute did a great deal to improve the quality of life in the rural communities in which it operated. Its members found their work to be a source of personal satisfaction and an outlet for their abilities and talents. Through participation they learned from one another, had fun doing so and developed friendships through the pursuit of a common cause.

Another major contribution of women to the community was made through participation in hospital auxiliaries. The magnitude of their contribution to hospital improvement is illustrated in a description of the work of the Ladies Auxiliary of the Aberdeen Hospital in New Glasgow, which was organized to aid the executive of the hospital in 1896.[29] The members performed a wide range of activities to raise funds for the hospital; they catered suppers, luncheons, dinners and teas, held pantry sales and raffled quilts and Christmas dinners. The money the women raised was used to purchase furniture and equipment for the hospital. The women helped to make life more enjoyable for the patients and staff by providing Thanksgiving and Christmas dinners. Rural women helped the Aberdeen auxiliary by providing poultry, eggs, bacon, butter, vegetables, currants, berries, jams, skeins of yarn, magazines and books, as well as some cash. In the early 1950s, much

93

Fig. 28 Hospital fundraiser at the Harris House, 1915. Courtesy Antigonish Heritage Museum. 2003.031.001.

of the bedding for hospital wards and linens for the operating room were made by members of the auxiliary.[30] They provided a bookmobile to serve hospital patients and they were instrumental in advocating for maternity services which resulted in the equipping of the hospital's obstetrical facilities. Auxiliaries throughout eastern communities did similar work.

Women and War

The two world wars forever changed the lives of Highland Scottish women in eastern Nova Scotia and Cape Breton. The departure of many of their husbands for war left them to bring up their children alone, and for some the obligation became permanent. Women's largest contribution to the war effort was through their unpaid labour in the home and through their voluntary activities.[31] They took time away from their household and farm duties to prepare boxes to be sent to the men away at war and to help the Red Cross provide aid to the soldiers in the field of battle.

The respect women won for their contribution on the home front during World War I had political consequences. Their contribution aroused considerable public sympathy for suffrage, and the result was the passage of the War-time Elections Act of 1917 which gave the right to vote in a federal election to women who were

British subjects, twenty-one years of age or older, and who had a close relative serving in the armed forces of Britain or Canada.[32] An advertisement in the *Halifax Herald* designed to get the attention of female voters in Nova Scotia in the 1918 Federal Election reflects public appreciation of the contributions of women:

> For over three years you have worked without ceasing in making and sending comforts to your boys in the trenches. You have sacrificed social pleasures, have greatly upset the routine of your homes, in many cases have skimped and connived to make the lot of our fighting lads happier away out there in the Battlefields.[33]

The Women's Franchise Act of 1919 broadened the right to vote in a federal election to include women twenty-one years of age or older who were British subjects, removing the stipulation of relations of servicemen. In 1920 the Dominion Elections Act provided universal suffrage. Women won the right to vote in provincial elections in Nova Scotia in 1918.

During World War II the Department of National Defense appealed to homemakers for specific kinds of assistance in the war effort. Advertisements appeared in the local papers asking women to save cooking fats, used to prepare glycerine for high explosives, and these were turned over to a local volunteer salvage committee. One of these appeals read: "Every Canadian kitchen can become an arsenal these days if even the smallest drops of used fats are saved."[34] War-time propaganda urged women to contribute to the war effort by encouraging their children to buy war-savings stamps and by urging their husbands to buy victory bonds. An advertisement in a local newspaper of 1941 stated: "Urge your menfolk to buy victory bonds now."[35]

Women also contributed to the war effort by living within the limits rationing imposed, by reducng waste and by saving and collecting materials that could be recycled in the war manufacturing industry.[36] Rationing made it difficult to produce the range and quantity of food the family diet required, particularly in urban areas. In 1943 meat joined sugar, butter, tea and coffee as rationed foods.[37] Urban women increased Canada's food production by cultivating victory gardens to provide fresh vegetables for the table. They also canned produce from the garden for use in the winter months.

The end of the war brought about a marked improvement in the lives of many Highland women because it brought increased prosperity that lasted through the fifties. Because of this prosperity, most women's economic role shifted from producer to consumer. Prosperity meant that more families could afford expensive products such as cars, furniture and appliances. A review of magazines between 1935 and 1950 reveals that the majority of advertisements were directed toward homemakers and that they promoted products primarily on the basis of their ability to reduce the drudgery of housework and to save time. Advertisements both created and catered to women's demands by painting "rosy pictures of an appliance-filled future."[38] Women recalled how wonderful they thought it was to be able to have store-bought baked goods, to purchase, rather than to make, clothing for the family and to be able to buy new furniture and appliances. As women came to rely more on store-bought food, traditional Highland fare was prepared only for special occasions. These changes led to the decline of many of the traditional household arts that were part of the Highland folk culture.

World War II had raised the demand for farm products and this increased income, besides creating new buying power, altered farm life. Tensions sometimes developed between men and women over the use of money. Men preferred to use the money to purchase farm machinery, while women wished to use it for home improvement. The gradual change from self-sufficiency to dependence on the cash economy, which had been under way for some time, was accelerated by the war. Labour-saving devices altered women's traditional domestic activities and women's work on the farm was reduced and in many cases terminated. While rural women did not increase their participation in the labour force during the war, urban women did, and this was a major impetus behind the increasing number of women working outside the home since that time. World War II marked a turning point in the lives of the Highland Scottish women of eastern Nova Scotia and Cape Breton.

Seven

Life in the Industrial Areas

The movement of Highland Scots to industrialized areas in eastern Nova Scotia and Cape Breton was part of a larger North American pattern of migration from rural areas to urban areas. Younger family members tended to migrate when family size increased and the farms were incapable of supporting them. Some Highland women found themselves caught up in the forces of industrialization because of employment decisions of their husbands. The first industrialized area in eastern Nova Scotia was Pictou County. Even while the immigration of Highland Scots to eastern Nova Scotia was still in progress, coal was being mined in Pictou County. By the 19th century, coal mining became a major industry in Pictou County and Cape Breton, and the steel industry developed in these areas in conjunction with coal. The move to the industrial areas brought a way of life vastly different from that in rural communities.

Life in the Mining Communities

In the late 19th century, industrialization created the first major demand for coal,[1] and coal mining expanded to become the dominant industry in Pictou County for 120 years.[2] While other industries waxed and waned, coal mining was a consistent source of livelihood between 1830 and 1950. The main mining towns in Pictou County were Stellarton, Westville and Thorburn.

Cape Breton and Inverness counties also had large deposits of coal, and coal mining operations in Cape Breton began in earnest in the 1830s with the opening of a mine in Sydney Mines by the General Mining Association.[3] Mining towns developed at Sydney Mines, Reserve, Glace Bay-Donkin, Port Morien, New Waterford, Dominion and Inverness. All the mining towns tended to be one-industry towns making them entirely dependent on the coal industry for jobs and livelihoods. Once the mines were developed in these towns, the coal industry became by far the largest single employer in the province of Nova Scotia.[4] There were approximately fifteen collieries in eastern Nova Scotia and, at its peak, the coal industry employed more than 13,000 people. Young Highland Scots migrated from the surrounding rural areas to all three counties—Pictou, Cape Breton and Inverness—in such numbers that they came to constitute the majority of the miners. They either brought their families with them or they went back for them after they got settled.

Highland wives in the mining communities were faced with a way of life heretofore foreign to them. They lost their partnership in the production of goods and services needed by the family, and to a large extent they became economically dependent on their husbands; in a cash economy productivity was limited primarily

Fig. 29 A row of company houses in Florence, Cape Breton. Photo by: NFB, c.1940s. Beaton Institute. 96-1025-27713.

*Fig. 30 A row house in Sydney Mines. Photo by: NFB, c.1940s Beaton Institute.
99-1021-27709.*

to work that drew a wage. Women's primary economic role shifted
from producer to consumer, but some women retained a measure
of domestic income by keeping some livestock and growing vegetables for home consumption. Others raised extra cash by selling
baked goods, taking in laundry, keeping boarders and by maintaining various forms of practical arts like weaving.[5]

The mining company owned most of the miners' homes, most
of the stores and it controlled the allocation of a large part of the
miners' income. Eighty per cent of mining families lived in the
company houses[6] that were built in large numbers in the Pictou
and Sydney fields. In Inverness, dozens of company houses were
built during the first two decades of the 20th century.[7] The General
Mining Association built one-storey row dwellings along the roads
adjacent to the mine sites in Albion Mines and in Sydney Mines,[8]
and boarding houses were built for single men. In Cape Breton
the houses were painted dark colors such as green or brown
which gave them a somber appearance. In Pictou and Inverness,

the row houses were called "red rows" because of their deep red paint. Row houses predominated until the 1890s, when two-storey double homes became the most common style. By 1900, Glace Bay had one thousand new double homes.[9]

The greatest period of building occurred between 1890 and 1914 when the mining companies constructed approximately 3500 houses near the coal fields and rented them to the miners.[10] In Inverness, miners were housed in relatively large, two-storey, double homes containing six rooms—three downstairs and three upstairs. The most spacious of all the company houses were those erected by the Acadia Coal Company at Albion Mines, later known as Stellarton. Many were double houses, each with a kitchen, dining room, and living room downstairs and four bedrooms upstairs. In the Sydney field, where the largest number of houses was built, the most common design was a two-storey double house with six rooms on each side. The exterior walls were shingles or clapboard, and the interior walls were plaster. Originally these houses were built without basements. Because they were so close together and because the walls were paper thin, there was little privacy. Some mining families abhorred this lack of privacy; others saw it as an asset because they enjoyed the closeness of social contact it encouraged.[11]

Company houses in the Sydney field rapidly deteriorated, and locals often referred to them as "shacks." The Royal Commission on Coal, in 1925, reported myriad complaints of leaky roofs, ill-fitting, doors and windows, rotten or badly worn floors and poor paper and plaster on the walls.[12] Because the company owned the houses, the families who occupied them felt little responsibility to repair them or even to make them look attractive. The Commissioners noted that similar complaints were not made about the houses built in Pictou County, because these houses were considered to be better quality.

The burden of housework was exacerbated by the limited availability of public utilities in the mining communities.[13] Before running water was supplied to mining towns in Cape Breton in 1904, water was either delivered by the mine operators or carried from wells or brooks by the women and children. Even those who had running water did not have indoor bathroom facilities because of the lack of sewers. Edith Stewart of Sydney Mines remembers that her mother lived in a house without indoor facilities. "Life in town without these facilities was very hard," she said. The toilet was a privy behind the house, and the "honey man" came once a year to empty it. Water was drained from the house into the ditch along the street, and the stench in warm weather was overwhelming.[14] Most houses did not receive electricity until the 1920s or 1930s and sewerage until after 1945.[15] The streets were often badly rutted and poorly lighted.

Though lack of public utilities was a problem in many towns in eastern Nova Scotia, it was more pressing in the mining communities because of the closeness of the houses, the large number of people who occupied them and the dirt and the dust from the street combined with the ever-present coal dust. This was the environment in which the women spent most of their lives. For women who came from the surrounding countryside where they were used to a clean environment and fresh air, getting used to the environment of the mining community was quite an adjustment—especially for those who thought life would be better away from the hardscrabble rural farms.

A few miners in Pictou County and Cape Breton did own small farms in areas close to the mining towns.[16] Women and children took primary responsibility for growing vegetable gardens and looking after livestock that usually consisted of a few cows, a few sheep, a pig and some chickens. These farms gave the mining families a degree of independence from the mining company, as well as fresh air and plenty of food. Realizing their advantages over the people living in the mining towns, those with farms willingly shared some of their surplus food with fellow miners and their families in times of adversity. Sr. Jean Grant, of Linacy, remembers "how her father used to hunt moose to provide meat to share with people in need."

The miners' salaries and company-provided expenses were allocated through the check-off system, which was established in 1880. The check-off system was used to set aside a portion of each miner's salary at the source, to cover the cost of most of the family's domestic expenses and some costs pertaining to employment. These expenses included rent for the company house, groceries and other household supplies from the company store, coal for stoves and furnaces, public utilities, union dues, hospital, doctor and church, contributions to the employees benefit fund and supplies for work from the company warehouse.[17] Because of these deductions, some miners referred to their pay cheques as the "bob-tail sheet," that is, the paycheque with the tail end cut off because the miner had no wage coming to him.

When work in the mines was irregular, and this was a frequent occurrence, the deductions from the miners' pay cheques ranged from 50 to 100 per cent of their weekly earnings.[18] Complaints increased as the amount of the salary chewed up by the deductions increased. The son of an Inverness miner, Donald Gillis, recalled how his father carried a cheque in his shirt pocket for years as a grim reminder of the control of the company over his life. "My father worked for two weeks only to find that the deductions left him with a pay cheque of just one cent."

The greatest support for the check-off system came from the wives of miners who drank heavily, because the deductions meant that at least the cost of the basic necessities would be covered. But Sr. Mary MacDonald, a former social worker in industrial Cape Breton, had a different view of the consequences of the check-off system: "This and other controls the company exercised over the lives of the miners lessened their sense of responsibility." While the check-off system was controversial, it was an efficient means of allocating payments.

In the mining communities in industrial Cape Breton, most of the purchasing was done at the company store and, according to Donald Gillis, it was the women who did the buying. The company store was usually a two-storey building with the first floor used for groceries and the second floor for furniture and clothing. The prices were reasonable, and the quality of the goods was satisfactory. When women bought groceries and other necessities for the household, the bill was deducted from their husbands' pay sheets. Saturday morning and evening were the busiest times at the company store and mothers often took their children shopping with them to make the expedition a happy social occasion. Nobody was in a rush to finish shopping, for the store was a meeting place for everyone in the community. The wives of men with a good credit record were able to obtain on credit everything their families needed during the slack season. Even as alternatives to company stores developed, many continued to shop at the company stores because they were known to carry quality goods and to give fair measure. The stores also provided jobs and business experience for the sons and daughters of many miners. In the mining communities in Pictou County, groceries stores had delivery services. Food could also be obtained from farmers and butchers who peddled their goods from door to door.[19] The women supplemented what they bought from the company store with purchases from Eaton's catalogue, if they had enough money, but usually there were few discretionary funds. Ever mindful of the irregularity of employment in the mines, the women tended to be frugal.

Coal mining was a distinctive way of life. It provided a bond drawing all mining families together, and the lives of wives and children revolved around coal mining. As Agnes MacKinnon from New Victoria put it, "The long arm of the mine reached into the homes of the miners' wives. Their domestic routine was dictated by the shift work of their husbands, sons and boarders." Boarding houses were in demand when men were flocking to the mining towns during the early years of the 20th century, and to supplement their husbands' income wives often took in boarders. With family members and boarders working different shifts, women had to prepare meals both day and night. The wives of miners on day shift got up before dawn to get the men out to work.[20] They lit the fire in the kitchen stove, boiled water for tea and packed lunches, which usually consisted of sandwiches, sweets, tea and a bottle of milk. After their husbands left for work, the wives got the children up, fed them and got them ready for school. After the children were off, the women went about their daily work of washing, ironing, sewing, patching, darning, scrubbing, cleaning and cooking.

The women spent two full days of each week, usually Monday and Tuesday, looking after the wash, and this entailed heavy physical labour. They lifted water into copper boilers, which they had placed on the stove to be heated, poured this water into a washtub when it was hot and then they lathered the clothes with lye soap and rubbed them on a scrub board. Their husbands' pit clothes were caked with coal dust and had to be soaked before they were scrubbed. Women dried the clothes outside and often finished the process indoors. The clothes were frequently speckled with soot, coal and road dust before they were dry. The day after washing was devoted to patching, darning and ironing. After making necessary repairs to the clothing, the women heated two or three heavy irons on top of the kitchen stove and then ironed for two or three hours. At least twice a week before the wood was covered with oilcloth, which was easier to clean, the women scrubbed the wooden plank floors. The women washed the walls regularly to remove the grease and grime from coal-burning stoves and kerosene lamps.

The supply of food purchased for the home was usually limited to the basics: potatoes, flour, oatmeal, tea, sugar, molasses, seasonal vegetables and fruit and whatever amount of meat and fish they could afford. If wives had the ingredients, they prepared large hot meals for their husbands before and after work. Children of the miners remember that as the paycheque ran out, their mothers served more and more soup. Soup dishes were used frequently to stretch the meat, fish and vegetables when they were in short supply. Lorne MacLellan, the son of a miner from Sydney Mines, remembers how "the women had to learn to make do. It was amazing how they could make a meal out of almost nothing."

Needle work occupied a great deal of the time that miners' wives had left after the housework. Every article of clothing was used and reused. Edith Stewart, the wife of a miner from Sydney Mines, stated that "some mothers made all their children's clothes from old clothes." Clothes were handed down from one child to the next, and they were mended and patched until they could no longer be repaired. Flour bags were bleached and turned into clothing. When old clothes were no longer fit to wear, the women cut them into pieces to be made into quilts and mats.

Most of the women's social activities took place in the home and were, for the most part, an extension of their housework.[21] Sometimes they took their sewing or knitting to a friend's house where they would share conversation over a cup of tea while they worked. Some played cards with friends or family members.

The mining families that survived the best were those that could supplement the husband's cheque with home-grown products.[22] Farming activity was not confined to those who owned farms outside of town; even in the mining towns, where the soil was fertile enough for gardening, many families grew vegetables. Catherine Chisholm of Antigonish reported that women also did most of the gardening. She said people quipped that: "No man should plant a garden too large for his wife to attend." Miners who owned their own homes in town often had a cow, pigs and chickens to supplement the supply of food bought at the company store. These families built small barns, hen houses and pig sties behind their homes. Lorne MacLellan remembered that as a child, his mother often sent him with a large pitcher to the home of the nearest neighbour who owned a cow to get milk for the family. Many urban dwellers continued to keep livestock until this practice was outlawed by municipal by-laws enacted in the 1940s.

Most of the time, the mining industry was highly seasonal, and therefore daily earnings were not a good index of the income of coal miners.[23] In Cape Breton the summer was the busy season, and on the mainland it was the autumn and the winter. For the rest of the year, the miners often worked only one, two or three days a week. Donald Gillis, who grew up in the mining community of Inverness where work was often sporadic, described the measures miners took to carry them through the lean times:"During the seasons in which they worked, the miners who were good managers tried to save enough money to buy such staples as a side of pork, a barrel of herring, a bucket of dried cod fish and two or three bags of flour."They hoped such measures would help to make ends meet when employment was low and money was scarce.

Mining families tended to be large. Until the mid-thirties, babies were born at home, assisted by a doctor, nurse or mid-wife. Extensive interviews with miners' wives revealed their deep love for their children,[24] and their aspirations to be the best wives and mothers they could be. They would not hear of the children of deceased relatives going to orphanages; instead they folded them into their families. If a mother died, her aunt, sister, eldest daughter or a female relative of her husband usually looked after the children.

The aspirations of the miners and their wives for their children varied. Some wanted their sons to be miners because it was the only life they knew and it would keep them at home. Out of economic necessity many boys left school at a young age to go to work"in the pit."[25] With the permanent injury or death of a breadwinner, this was the only way a family could keep a roof over its head. There was an informal system of apprenticeship that allowed the sons of miners into the pits before they were eighteen to learn the skills of mining. Boys under the age of ten sometimes worked underground, before the Mines Act of 1873 prohibited anyone under ten in the mines.[26] In 1891 the Mines Act raised the minimum age for young miners to twelve. Descendants of the early miners believed that a boy's size had more to do with his getting a job than his age."If a boy was big for his age, he could get into the mines very young," said Donald Gillis, of Inverness. Boys in the mines did jobs not requiring the strength and experience of men, primarily working as trappers and drivers.[27] Trapping, often the first job assigned to boys, involved tending to the system of doors that controlled the mine ventilation system. Boys opened and shut the ventilation doors along the various underground passages so that drivers leading horses and mules hauling the coal boxes could pass.[28]

These boys provided a pool of cheap labour, since their wages were roughly 60 to 70 per cent of the adult miners. The juvenile workers represented approximately 20 per cent of the work force; at its high point in 1890 numbering 1,102 boys.[29] For many of these boys working in the mines was an early initiation into manhood. They took great pride in their early induction into the world of work, following in the footsteps of their fathers and winning respect at home. Child labour began to decline in the late 1800s when mechanical haulage reduced the number of horses underground; finally it disappeared after World War I.

Equally, there were many mothers and fathers who regarded mining as the last thing they wanted for their children.[30] Edith Stewart of Sydney Mines reflected this view when she said: "I dreaded seeing my husband go to the mine, and I certainly did not want this for my son." These parents saw no future in mining, and they vowed that their children would get an education and escape the mines. Education was viewed as the way to a better and easier life, and for these parents, no sacrifice was too large when it came to getting their children an education. Cyril Grant reported that in his home town of Inverness, "members of the community from all walks of life joined forces with parents in counselling the young people to stay in school." There was no future in the mines for these young people because the mines only operated sporadically. Lorne MacLellan said that it was his Calvinist mother who emphasized that he should get an education; her religious beliefs held that success was a mark of God's favour. The Protestant work ethic had a strong influence on many women and they transmitted this influence to their children.

Most daughters followed in their mothers' footsteps by learning the skills of housekeeping both at home and in domestic science courses in school. A girl was socialized to the roles of miner's wife and mother of his children as she helped her own mother maintain a mining household.[31] Most families considered learning to be a homemaker the most important part of a girl's education. After leaving school many young women remained at home to help their mothers until they married or went out to work. If they did not have an education beyond high school, the only options for them outside the home were working as housekeepers or store clerks. Adventurous young women made their way to Massachusetts to work as housekeepers, and in some cases were encouraged by their families to leave. The education of the sons was a much higher priority than the education of daughters, but some mining families were ambitious for their daughters as well, and they managed to send them to nursing school, teachers college or to university.

Highland women and men in the mining towns remained in touch with their rural roots and they retained their Highland cultural traditions.[32] Living in relative proximity to their rural homes reinforced this orientation. Because the majority of the miners and their wives were Highland Scots, folk tradition played an important part in the social life of the mining communities.[33] Gaelic songs and tales were a prominent feature of ceilidhs and concerts. Old as well as new songs and tales were heard at social gatherings, union meetings, political gatherings, in the tavern, on street corners and in the mine yards, washrooms and pits. Some of the Gaelic songs composed and sung in urban Cape Breton reflected the problems of the mining community. From Glace Bay in the 1920s came this lament penned in Gaelic by a local bard.

> Oh, isn't it a shame for a healthy Gael living in this place to be a slave from Monday to Saturday under the heels of tyrants, when he could be happy on a handsome spreading farm with milk-cows, white sheep, hens, horses, and perhaps a car, and clean work on the surface of the earth, rather than in the black pit of misery.[34]

Until the 1920s, Gaelic conversation was heard in the streets and in the washhouses of the coal companies in Cape Breton, and special Gaelic services were held in the Catholic and Presbyterian churches, but the Gaelic language declined more quickly in multicultural urban areas than in the rural communities. From the 1920s, English became the common language for people of diverse ethnic origins as well as the language of business.

The adversity the miners faced had a deep impact on their families. Miners' wives were keenly aware of the danger their husbands and sons faced in the mines and they lived with the specter of death hanging over them. The presence of methane gas in the mines was particularly dangerous. Between 1838 and 1952, 246 miners were killed in explosions in Pictou County alone.[35] Explosions in the Allan Shaft, long considered one of the most dangerous mines in the world, took the lives of 101 men between 1914 and 1935, 88 of them in 1918 in the worst mine disaster in Pictou County. In this explosion some women lost two or more family members from the ranks of their fathers, brothers, husbands and sons.

Many other miners were killed by falling rocks, falling coal and roof cave-ins which trapped them underground. Some were run over by coal cars. Paralleling the high death rate was a high injury rate. Poor health was another price miners paid for working in the mines, and many miners developed black lung disease from the coal dust and poor ventilation in the mines. Miners' complaints about these problems were often ignored. A report on the state of conditions in the mines in Nova Scotia concluded that unsafe and unsatisfactory working conditions have always been characteristic of the coal industry.[36] The accidental death rate among coal miners was higher than in any other occupation of similar size and nature,[37] but the owners of the coal companies turned a blind eye to these problems. Miners who complained about working conditions were often dismissed from their jobs and then blacklisted to prevent them from getting jobs in other mines or in the steel plant.[38]

Experience taught the miners' wives to harbour a nagging worry about the safety of their spouses. Rod Ferguson, the son of a miner from Dominion, noted that "these women lived in fear." Children of miners recall growing up with the vivid picture in their minds of women racing frantically to the pit head as soon as they heard the sound of the pit whistle signalling an accident. When a man was killed in the mine, every woman in the mining community could identify with his wife—all feared the same fate for their men.[39]

The people of mining communities were warm and generous in their support of the wives and widows of accident victims and their families, but their meager resources limited their ability to help; the death of many miners resulted in grinding poverty for their families. Relief societies and benefit societies were started in the late 1800s, and they provided a small weekly payment to miners unable to work due to injury or illness and a death benefit for widows of miners with children.[40] Further assistance came in 1917 with the introduction of Workmen's Compensation. In either case the benefits were small. If a widow did not have a son old enough to go into the pit, she had to find some kind of work, and widows who did not have a family member working in the mines were forced out of the company houses. Some widows were able to obtain work cooking and cleaning in the houses of professional and business people in the community or in public institutions. Others took in laundry or baked goods to be delivered to their customers. A few superior cooks catered to family and public events. Some worked as seamstresses. They did whatever they could to survive.

Apart from a mine accident, the most stressful event in the lives of the miners' wives was a strike. Strikes made them fear for the safety of their husbands and the well-being of their children. Some of the most bitterly fought strikes in Canada occurred in Springhill, in Inverness and at the Dominion Coal Company's collieries in the Sydney field between 1909 and 1911.[41] During the strikes, miners were evicted from their company houses and many families returned to their rural homes. For those who did not have family nearby, the situation was desperate; many had no choice but to live in tents facing the specter of starvation. Adding to their despair was the church's lack of sympathy or support for their cause. Devout miners and wives were greatly distressed by the failure of the churches to respond compassionately to their plight. This situation began to change around 1920 when Fr. Jimmy Tompkins and other religious leaders in the Diocese of Antigonish stressed the need for social justice for miners and their families. Fr. Tompkins viewed education to be the key to improving the living and working conditions of the miners, and to that end he called for a vigorous program of adult education to bring knowledge to the people.[42] Bishop Morrison of the Diocese of Antigonish commented that "present economic conditions are bringing about a great social awakening among all classes of people."[43]

Conflict between the workers and management reached its most bitter phase between 1920 and 1925. The British Empire Steel Corporation, which controlled both the mines and the steel companies, announced several pay reductions which undermined

Fig. 31 A squadron of the Royal Canadian Dragoons ready for action during the Sydney steelworkers strike of 1925. Photo by: Unknown. Beaton Institute. 87-964-17494.

the livelihood of the miners and precipitated several strikes. With BESCO's wage reductions, miners' wives saw their families cut off from even the bare necessities of life. In 1925 the work force of ten thousand miners in Cape Breton and on the mainland reacted by walking out and staying out for five months to protest wage cuts and to demand improvements in working conditions. In retaliation BESCO suspended credit at its company stores.[44] A former nursing sister at the Hamilton Memorial Hospital, Sr. Mary Campbell, reported her father's reaction to the suspension of credit: "My father, the manager of a company store in New Waterford, known as 'Pluck-me Joe,' could not stand to see the miners' families go hungry and so, under the cover of darkness, he threw food out the store window to miners and their children." With the authority of the Federal Militia Act, 950 troops were sent to Cape Breton to keep order. A curfew was imposed on the mining communities, and if people did not obey it, the militia rode their horses beside them on the street and nudged them to go home. Edith Stewart of Sydney Mines recalled how the militia struck fear in the children: "Some of the soldiers even went so far as to threaten the miners' children

110

by riding their horses into the water where they were swimming in the ocean near Glace Bay."

The miners' families suffered terribly, and women went to desperate lengths to keep their families from starving. Even before the 1925 strike, employment was so irregular that many families were on the verge of starvation, and it was reported that in the Cape Breton coal fields some mothers "were feeding a soup boiled up from potato peelings flavored with droppings from a communal soup bone passed from house to house."[45] The strike spread from industrial Cape Breton to the mainland, and within three months many families there were on relief. Hunger was the most serious problem, and the Salvation Army set up soup kitchens in Cape Breton and in Pictou County for school children. Religious denominations set up relief stations to distribute donated food, but it was not sufficient to meet the needs of the miners' families. Having witnessed first hand the large number of people who were on the verge of starvation in 1925, Bishop James Morrison of the Diocese of Antigonish issued a letter to his parishioners calling for help in the relief of distress in the mining communities.[46] The diocesan clergy reinforced this appeal for help. They also helped with the work of the citizens' relief committees in establishing relief stations to distribute food and clothing, and the surrounding farming communities provided generous donations of food.

The wives of former miners remember the fear that gripped their homes as they found themselves without food. By mid-February 1925, a Glace Bay health officer reported that two thousand idle miners and their families were on the verge of starvation. When the miners became desperate, the confrontation with the police turned violent and resulted in the death of one miner and the wounding of several others. In retaliation, the miners burned a colliery and a wash house and started twenty-two incendiary fires. When the company continued to refuse to allow the miners to obtain food on credit, hungry angry miners looted the company stores.[47] The women helped the men carry away barrels of sugar, bags of flour, canned goods and other food items. Some store managers who could not stand to see people going without food did not try to stop them. The demise of the company stores is colourfully described by one of the looters: "They were burned to the ground, every one of them. I helped to do it. It was an act of desperation. It took us three nights to clean them stores out. The third night they put a match to it. They burned them all."[48] As public sympathy swung to the side of the miners, the new Conservative government persuaded the company and the miners to accept a compromise settlement involving an agreement to a small wage reduction and the promise of a Royal Commission to study the coal industry.[49]

The company made no effort to re-establish the stores that had burned; they were replaced by private stores and co-operative stores. The large mining town of Sydney Mines saw the arrival of an Eaton's department store with a groceteria, and the Extension Department of St. Francis Xavier University helped in the formation of co-operative stores owned and controlled by the miners.

After 1925 the mining companies started offering to sell the company houses to their tenants. For miners and their wives who were keenly aware of the deterioration of these houses, this was not an attractive option. Furthermore, because of the uncertainty of employment and income, those who were interested could not obtain the credit needed to finance their purchase. As the condition of the company houses worsened, families began to look for other options.[50] The Extension Department of St. Francis Xavier University provided leadership in helping miners build and own their own homes. Fr. Jimmy Tompkins, who was then parish priest in Reserve Mines, spearheaded efforts to organize the miners to build co-operative houses. The miners' wives were also eager participants in this endeavour.[51] Under Fr. Tompkins' guidance, miners in Reserve Mines came up with a group system for building houses on a co-operative basis, and their efforts resulted in the establishment of the first co-operative housing project in eastern Canada, at Tompkinsville on the outskirts of Reserve Mines. Tompkins's encouragement and inspiration strengthened their resolve to persevere in this endeavour. Miners' wives not only took part in study clubs, but in the work of building the houses as well. They worked alongside their husbands, carrying tools and lumber to them and sometimes nailing floors and shingling roofs and walls. It was a great day when Tompkinsville was formally opened in 1938.[52]

The Depression of the 1930s brought renewed hardship to mining families. Reduced demand for coal led to a high rate of unemployment, and the coal companies responded to the loss of markets by reducing the number of shifts. During this period miners were lucky to get a couple of shifts a week. Every day the men and women listened for the whistle. "If it blew two, there was no work. If it was a long whistle, there was work."[53] Many miners had to depend on small municipal relief payments to keep their families alive, and others rode the rails from town to town in a desperate bid to find work. Life was particularly bleak for the wives and children of miners who lived in Inverness where the coal seams were running out. Everything from the food on the table to medical services depended on whether or not the father was working.

Mining recovered briefly during World War II, only to decline again after the war.[54] High costs of mining coal made it uncompetitive against cheap oil, and the demand for coal diminished greatly when the Canadian National Railway stopped using it. Between 1947 and 1957, four of the main mines in Pictou County and the mines in Inverness closed; in industrial Cape Breton coal mining operations were reduced in scale. The once great mining industry was but a shadow of its former self, and many miners left the mining communities in the late 1940s and 1950s. The era of the mining community and the distinctive, if unpredictable, way of life it created—not only for the miners but also for their wives and children—had come to an end. The Highland Scots who had moved from their tenuous rural life now found themselves alienated from the way of life of the mining towns as well.

Life in the Steel Towns

Just as the young Highland Scots from rural communities migrated to the coal fields in eastern Nova Scotia and Cape Breton, they also moved to the steel towns. And, just like the coal miners, many brought with them or returned for young Scottish brides from the countryside. And like coal mining, the women as well as the men found their lives to be highly contingent.

The Canadian steel industry was born in Pictou County,[55] when the Nova Scotia Steel Company was formed in 1882. From its furnaces came the first steel ingots produced in Canada.[56] This company, located in Trenton, expanded by taking over several other related companies in 1895 and became a major source of employment in Pictou County.[57] The Nova Scotia Steel Company decided to expand again, this time by establishing new iron and steel furnaces near the coal mines in Sydney Mines, Cape Breton.

What was to become the most important steel center in eastern Nova Scotia developed in Sydney where the steel operation

113

was a direct outgrowth of the coal industry.[58] At the turn of the century, Sydney was a small community that was not prepared to handle a large increase in population. Just as had occurred in Pictou County, the growth of the steel industry in Sydney brought an influx of young men and women from the countryside, most of whom were Highland Scots. It also brought immigrants from Europe, the United States and Newfoundland. With this influx the population of Sydney rose from 3200 in 1899 to 17,723 in 1911.[59] Pronounced class divisions developed between Canadian-born workers and immigrants. The Black, Italian, Eastern European and Newfoundland immigrants occupied the bottom of the social ladder,[60] and they were the victims of discrimination at work and in the community. They were hired for the least desirable and lowest paying jobs and were over-represented in the demanding, dirty and unskilled work in the coke ovens and blast furnaces.[61] Foreign labour was in excess of 75 per cent at the blast furnaces and close to 85 per cent at the coke ovens.[62]

On the other hand, Canadian-born workers, including Highland Scots, tended to get the better-paying and more skilled jobs at the steel plant. These class divisions did not occur in Pictou County because the steel plant located there did not attract a large number of foreign workers. The industrial activities in Pictou County were on a smaller scale than those in Cape Breton, and a sufficient supply of labour could be obtained from men who moved in from the farms.[63]

The social distance that existed between the Canadian steel workers and the immigrants in Sydney was reinforced by the housing policy of the steel company. Because of the shortage of housing in Sydney, the steel company built company houses,[64] but it provided different classes of housing for different classes of workers. For those with better jobs the company built bigger and better houses in cleaner and more attractive parts of the city. For the Canadian-born workers the company built small but well-appointed single-family houses. The wives of the Canadian-born steel workers, including most of the wives of the Highland Scottish workers, expressed satisfaction with the housing situation. The immigrant workers, on the other hand, got the poorest quality housing and lived in the most squalid conditions. The company located thirty-eight Ukrainian, Hungarian and Polish families on its own property beside the steel plant.[65] It built nine single, two, three and four-storey family houses on 1.5 acres (.6 hectares). The provision of public utilities in these areas, including electricity, water and sewerage, lagged behind the rest of the city.

The wives and children of immigrants who lived beside the steel plant and in the area adjoining the coke ovens suffered from overcrowding and lack of sanitation that led to serious health problems.[66] Typhoid fever was rampant, and mothers feared for the lives of their children. Their alarm was well founded, for illnesses claimed approximately 20 per cent of the infants in Sydney before they were two months old. Dirt spewing from the coke ovens contributed to poor sanitation. When water was put on the hot coals to make coke, the ovens belched dirty steam which spewed over the surrounding areas. The women who lived by the coke ovens and its immediate surroundings said that when the wind blew these unhealthy emissions in their direction, a smog hung over the area that soiled their laundry. Betty Andrews, the wife of a steel worker, recalled that "if you lived in the area close to the coke ovens, you had to know which way the wind was blowing before you put your clothes on the line to dry."

Not all steel workers lived in company houses. Some built their own homes and this gave them a measure of independence from the steel company that those living in company houses did not feel. Some purchased small farms on the outskirts of the city to raise livestock and grow their own gardens, and the women enjoyed working on the farms with their husbands. The produce the farm provided supplemented the husband's income, making some like Marie MacDonald, the daughter of a steel worker from East Bay, feel that, "We were prosperous."

The steel industry was characterized by intermittent periods of prosperity and depression.[67] The steel plants tended to boom during war time and to decline when war was over. By 1912 the Dominion Steel and Coal Company was an industrial giant producing 50 per cent of all the steel consumed annually in Canada,[68] but very little of the profit trickled down to the workers. In the first two decades of the 20th century, the steel workers received low wages and toiled in poor working conditions.[69] Great unrest was precipitated by unfulfilled promises of better pay and improved working conditions. Accidents occurred daily because of unsafe working conditions and exhaustion from overwork. Irene MacDonald, the daughter of a steel worker, stated that, "The wives of the men who worked around the blast furnaces harboured a nagging fear that their husbands would get burned."Their insecurity was heightened by the fact that there were no benefits for workers who missed work because of injury or illness, and the company had no pension plan. Assistance for accident victims came primarily from fellow workers who took up collections for them.

> The first steel strike in Sydney occurred in 1903, and discrimination against immigrant workers carried over into this strike.[70] Families of Highland Scottish women who married immigrants have kept alive the stories of life during this strike. Because the strike was initiated by Italians and Hungarians, the Anglo-Saxon dominated Provincial Workers Association did not come to the aid of the strikers, even when they were subjected to beatings, evictions and blacklisting. The threat these measures posed to the safety, security and livelihood of the steel workers aroused great anxiety in their wives and children.

In 1920, the Dominion Steel Corporation and the Nova Scotia Steel and Coal Company came together to form the British Empire Steel Corporation. Financial trouble throughout this company's existence was at the root of labour strife in the 1920s.[71] Plant closures, lay-offs and wage cuts created unrest that led to a major strike in 1923. The Nova Scotia government moved quickly to come to the aid of the company[72] by hastily recruiting a provincial police force and persuading the federal government to send in the militia. This happened despite the fact that the great majority of the steel workers were neither radical nor reactionary. The company used the excuse of communist plotting by the workers to justify punitive measures[73] and brought in the police and the militia to intimidate the workers. Witnesses complained of harsh and unwarranted treatment of workers by the provincial police.[74] The steel company officials viewed the gathering of the workers around the Sydney plant on Sunday, July 1, 1923, as an unlawful assembly, and they called on the provincial police to disperse the workers. It was difficult for the police to distinguish strikers from other citizens of the community, and the police made a terrible error by attacking unarmed strikers and their families returning from church. The attack on innocent people is remembered to this day as Bloody Sunday.[75] This description of the event comes from an open letter submitted to the press by J. B. MacLaughlan, head of District 26 of the United Mine Workers of America:

On Sunday night last these provincial police, in the most brutal fashion, rode down the people at Whitney Pier who were on the street, most of whom were coming from church. Neither age, sex, nor physical disability was proof against these brutes. One old woman, over seventy years of age, was beaten into insensibility and may die. A boy nine years old was trampled under the horses' feet and had his breastbone crushed in. One woman, beaten over the head with a police club, gave premature birth to a child. The child is dead and the woman's life is despaired of. Men and women were beaten up inside their own homes.[76]

A description of the incident written by the Royal Canadian Mounted Police was less graphic than MacLaughlan's, but even the RCMP admitted that a number of innocent people were injured. Even though reports of the event varied, there was agreement that the police went too far.

These excesses aroused the anger of the broader labour community[77] and the strike escalated when the miners of Cape Breton and Pictou responded by striking in sympathy with the Sydney steelworkers.[78] The anxiety of steel-workers families was increased by BESCO's announcement that it was going to evict the strikers and their families from their company houses. This threat, combined with the depletion of their resources, limited work and repeated cuts in wages, forced the strikers to give up their cause and return to work, but it did not end the anxiety of the wives and families of the leading union activists. After the workers agreed to call off the strike, the company found excuses to fire and blacklist the activists so that they could not obtain employment in the steel plant or in the coal fields. They found themselves without work and, in many cases, without a home and they had no choice but to leave the area in search of employment.

Steel workers and families were hit hard by the Depression. In 1931-32 the company shut down almost the entire steel operation, and during the remainder of the Depression the plant operated only intermittently. Most of the workers in Sydney and in Trenton were laid off and had to live on relief.[79] Each day they would go to the plant looking for a shift, usually to return home without work. A fortunate few managed to get one or two shifts a week. Workers who came from the surrounding rural communities often went home to their parents in hard times where they trapped, hunted and fished to help feed their own and other families.

This economic situation changed with the coming of World War II when the steel industry boomed. Workers received large increases in salary, and families remember that they lived very well during this period. The shortage of male workers during the war created an opportunity for women to work in the steel plant. Sixty-nine women worked in the Sydney steel plant between 1941 and 1945,[80] and those who obtained this work were delighted with the experience.[81] A woman who worked as a checker reported that she made good money and that her friends thought she was rich. Female steelworkers wore coveralls, did physical labour and were as black and greasy as the men. Many parents objected to their daughters working at the mill because they did not view such labour as "women's work," but this did not deter them from working at the plant. The women uniformly agreed that they enjoyed the work and made good money, but they realized that their jobs were temporary; the social conventions of the time dictated that industrial jobs belonged to men. When the men came back from the war, the company let the women go and their jobs were given back to the men. Some conceded grudgingly.[82]

Unlike the mining communities of industrial Cape Breton, Sydney did not have company stores. Women did their shopping in small privately-owned shops where the service was personal and the friendly owners and staff made shopping an enjoyable social experience.[83] Some shops extended credit to their customers; others operated on a cash-and-carry basis. Betty Andrews, the wife of a steel worker remembers: "The owners made us feel so comfortable that we felt free to linger and chat." Some wives did not go to the grocery stores to shop, but instead placed their orders by telephone, and the store owner saw that the groceries were delivered to their homes—a great convenience for families who did not own a vehicle.

Because the jobs of the steel workers tended to be better-paying than those of the miners, steel worker families aspired to higher educational goals for their children. For daughters, some saw possibilities in the secretarial, teaching and nursing professions; for sons, many wanted a university education. Like mining families, very few wanted their sons to work at the steel plant.

As a consequence of discrimination, the immigrant steel workers and their families did not mix socially with the rest of the population of Sydney. Many Highland Scottish women did not understand the social dynamics at work here, and attributed the social withdrawal of the immigrants to their desire to keep to themselves. This isolation drew the immigrant population together and reinforced the cultures of the ethnic groups they represented. Marie MacDonald observed: "Each ethnic group engaged in lively celebrations of its traditions, and this kept its culture alive." On the other hand, the interaction of the Highland Scots with the residents of Sydney weakened the hold of the Highland folk culture on them. They continued to play Highland folk music, but they also adopted the music, songs and musical instruments that were in vogue in Sydney. Playing hymns and Scottish music on the organ was a popular pastime, and the accordion was added to their list of musical instruments, but the tradition of storytelling—carried over from the rural areas—was usually confined to the home.

Class differentiation extended to many community activities in Sydney. Even Highland Scottish steel workers and their wives understood that the golf club and other social clubs were for the social elite. Betty Andrews remembered that, "Because of our low status in the community, we were not welcome." As a result, they depended primarily on family gatherings for their social life. They did the kinds of things family members enjoy when they get together: chatting, singing, dancing, eating and drinking. Additionally, the wives of the steel workers turned to their churches and their extended families for socializing. They put on teas and suppers to raise money for charity and to defray parish expenses. Catering to these events gave the women a chance to socialize with one another. In Sydney, the steel workers and their families had access to the facilities of the Young Men's Christian Association (YMCA) where women as well as men were welcome, and therefore the whole family could recreate together.

Unlike the miners' wives, most wives of the Highland Scottish steel workers had a positive view of the quality of life in the industrial areas. Except in times of strikes and economic depression, they were relatively secure and enjoyed a reasonably good standard of living. But like the coal industry, the steel industry started to decline in the late 1940s and the 1950s, a decline from which it never recovered. The permanent decay of these industries brought with it the demise of a way of life in eastern Nova Scotia and Cape Breton.

Eight

Women's Work Outside the Home

Before 1900, the opportunity for women to gain employment outside the home was limited—mainly domestic labour that was heavy and the wages low. A few women found work as milliners or dressmakers, producing goods for other women. As the rural communities shifted to a cash economy, and as urban and industrialized communities developed in the late-19th and early-20th century, the number of retail establishments increased, providing employment for women as retail clerks. Female clerks were usually required to work long hours for low wages, but many found their jobs satisfying, primarily because of the opportunity for social interaction they provided. Retail work also had the advantage of being less heavy than domestic labour, because most stores had owners or male employees who did the heavy lifting. A few women even opened their own stores. Many communities had a dress shop, a hat shop, a book store or a confectionary store owned and run by women, most of them single. Telephone service came to eastern Nova Scotia in the late 1800s, and this service provided employment opportunities for women as telephone operators.

Near the turn of the century, opportunities for employment in office work began to open up for women as stenographers, office clerks and secretaries,1 bringing large numbers of single women into the workforce.2 Before this time office work had been a male preserve, but when employers realized that they could get the same service for less money from women, clerical jobs became

Fig. 32 Millinery dept., Vooght's store, North Sydney, c.1914. Photo by: Unknown. Beaton Institute. 77-531-665.

predominantly female occupations. With the coming of shorthand and typing, women replaced men in clerical and secretarial occupations because they were thought to be more suited to work that was repetitive,[3] and less cerebral. Repetitive as office work was, it was viewed to be more glamorous and better paying than work as housekeepers or as store clerks.[4] The work was attractive because it was skilled, did not require heavy labour and previously had been the domain of men. Clerical and secretarial jobs represented a significant improvement in the job market for women, and after World War I there was a significant increase in office work, which served to make it generally more acceptable for women to work outside the home. Anticipating this increase in demand for office workers, private girls' schools offered courses in typing and shorthand to prepare young women for the increasingly gendered workforce.

Working outside the home was easier for women who lived in towns, of course, because of their proximity to places of employment. Young working women continued to live at home and handed over a portion or all of their earnings to their families.[5] The

121

money they made was often used to support ailing parents or wid-owed mothers. Their work also provided a welcome opportunity to get away from home and meet people outside their family, but it did not bring much freedom or independence. If young women did not live at home, they either lived with relatives near the job or boarded with a family, and in either situation they usually found themselves living within the confines of a protective family.

A sustained period of out-migration from rural parts of eastern Nova Scotia started in the 1880s,[6] caused initially by the Depression of the 1870s that marked the beginning of a long pe-riod of economic decline in the Maritimes. Travel was facilitated by the building of railways in the 1880s, which enabled workers to go west as well as to the New England states.[7] Adding to the depopulation was the large number of young men who lost their lives in World War I. When young Highland women found they outnumbered Highland men of marriageable age, they too left. Between 1881 and 1921, thousands of Highland Scottish women of Nova Scotia left for the New England states.[8] Stories of the prom-ise and prosperity of the New England states were brought back by their male relatives and friends who had found employment on New England fishing vessels sailing in and out of Massachusetts ports.[9] Hardest hit by depopulation in this period was Antigonish, where in 1919 there were 331 vacant farms.[10] The population of Antigonish County in 1881 was 18,060 and by 1921 it was reduced to 11,580.[11]

Women appeared to have had an even greater propensity to leave Nova Scotia than men.[12] With the establishment of busi-nesses by artisans and the opening of carding and spinning mills beginning in the late 1800s, household production declined, and the economic contribution of daughters to the home decreased accordingly. However, there was more to their leaving than social and economic conditions at home. Many women were motivated to leave by the lure of the city.[13] They developed romantic views of city life—from stories brought back first by men and later by wom-en who had moved to the New England states—that contrasted sharply with the isolation and austerity of rural life. In some cases women left because their families could no longer support them. At first many of those who left were lonely and longed to return home. Mae Smith from St. Andrews described the adjustment of these women: "While at first the young domestics who went to Boston were shy, scared and lonely, most went on to enjoy a good quality of life." There were also women who wanted to leave just long enough to obtain money for a trousseau and then return home to marry.

Boston became a symbol of the good life, and many were drawn to that city "as by a magnet."[14] Geographic accessibility also made Boston a convenient destination. Passage by steamer could be obtained from the ports of Halifax, Port Hawkesbury or Yarmouth. From 1865 to 1940, people travelled to Boston by train. Evidence of the amount of business created by travel to the New England states is reflected in the large number of advertisements for passage in local newspapers. A typical example in *The Casket* in 1890 advertised passage to Boston, Portland and Gloucester via the Intercolonial Railway and the Palace Steamer of the International Steamship Company which was leaving from the Strait of Canso.[15] Tony MacKenzie of Kenzieville reported that "women who could not afford to pay for their travel were often able to obtain passage on fishing schooners in return for their services as cooks and cleaners." So popular were the New England states as a destination for young people from Nova Scotia that *The Casket* in the early 1900s carried a column called "Boston Notes."

Paid Domestic Work

Women who went abroad found employment primarily in domestic service and, to a lesser degree, in clerical and retail jobs.[16] A few went into nursing and teaching. Those who planned to go into nursing usually spent some time working as housekeepers or in the retail trade in order to raise the necessary money for nursing school. They relied primarily on relatives already working in the U.S. to help them find jobs. The women who went into domestic service did not feel that the work gave them the inferior status so often associated with being a member of the serving class,[17] because many of them worked for wealthy families who provided much better working conditions than employers of domestic labour back home. Often, even as domestics, young women enjoyed greater freedom, prosperity and better living conditions than could be dreamed of at home. Mary Ann Boyd, of Lakevale, noted: "Some of the young women back home envied the domestics who worked for wealthy families." Coming as they did from communities where there were few employment opportunities for women, their jobs as housekeepers in wealthy homes looked very attractive. These women worked hard, lived well and were proud of their work—so were their families back home.

Housekeeping was a demanding job,[18] and women often worked from seven in the morning until seven in the evening. Sometimes, social events and special occasions made it necessary for them to work late into the evening and on days off, but employers usually compensated for additional demands by giving them extra pay or alternative time off. Their regular wages were sufficient to enable "the thrifty to save respectable sums of money."[19] Some former housekeepers talked of the pressure associated with preparing food and tables for social occasions and the holiday season; Christmas, they remembered, was particularly demanding.

Housekeepers were grateful for the opportunity to work in affluent homes, and many were in awe of the facilities available to them in these homes. For some it was their first experience with electric lights, electric appliances, central heating and indoor plumbing; they appreciated the convenience and comfort these facilities brought. They tended to be well accepted and respected by their employers, and often were treated as part of the family.[20] Many of their employers were genuinely concerned about their welfare, a situation very different from the master-servant relationship that characterized the terms under which the immigrant women of eastern Nova Scotia worked as indentured servants.

Coming as they did from quiet rural communities, these women revelled in the new experiences and independence available in the city. They found excitement in the opportunities the city provided for shopping, recreating and socializing. They had all of this without losing touch with their roots, because there were Down East clubs in Massachusetts where they went to mingle with people from home, converse in Gaelic, sing Scottish songs and dance to the music of the fiddle. In this social setting they could feel the warmth and cheer of their familiar Highland folk culture.

Women who were good letter writers would sometimes embellish the wonders of their life in the "Boston-States," a name given to all the American states by the Highland Scots of eastern Nova Scotia. They did not cease to be amazed at what the big city department stores had to offer or at the services brought to their doors by a variety of street vendors. Such stories encouraged other young women to join them in the New England states.

The wages that housekeepers received represented a substantial economic gain for women who did not come from a cash economy. These women rejoiced not only in having this money, but also in being able to control its dispersal. Furthermore, the value of this money was enhanced by the fact that housekeepers had virtually no living expenses, since employers provided food, shelter and uniforms. As a result, they were able to save what seemed like substantial amounts of money.

Even though these women were far from home, they retained a strong sense of family responsibility. The stories of how they used their money to help the folks back home are legion. Boxes and sometimes even barrels of second-hand clothing, clothing bought in bargain basements, or clothing given to them by the families for whom they worked, were sent home to be made over for their own families. Boxes of gifts were forwarded at Christmas. Monies were forwarded to the old folks to buy tobacco, candies, tea and other small luxuries. Frances MacIsaac of Brierly Brook recalled the words of one of her husband's relatives: "My pipe is full because my daughter keeps it full." Many families could not have gotten along without the generous assistance of these working women.

Ironically, some working women used their income to finance the education of male members of their families, making university education possible for many young men in Nova Scotia when their own education possibilities remained limited. Catholic women were known for their financial contributions to seminarians from their home communities to help cover the costs of their studies for the priesthood. Some made generous contributions to the churches in their home parishes.

When their employers went on vacation, they often gave the women time off and many used these days to go home. The stylish clothes they brought from the New England states were the envy of those used to homespuns. Their fine manners and fine speech were greeted with awe. But when they went too far with their city airs, awe quickly turned to derision. "Putting on airs was not well received," noted Betty Ballantyne, of Ballantynes Cove.

For some of these women their relationship with the families who employed them in the New England states continued long after they retired. This was reflected in the letters, photographs,

125

gifts and money sent to them by the women for whom they had worked. Many elderly women who had worked as housekeepers eagerly awaited correspondence from their former employers. Josephine MacIsaac from Antigonish remembered that "after Mary Ann Chisholm retired, her employer, Rose Kennedy, wrote to her on a regular basis. In her home at Malignant Cove, Mary Ann displayed proudly a signed photograph of John F. Kennedy that his mother forwarded to her on the occasion of her son's inauguration as president of the United States."

During and after World War II, more economic opportunities became available for Nova Scotia women. The Canadian Women's Army Corps recruited stenographers, typists, bookkeepers and laboratory technicians.[21] The men who went to war left behind jobs for women in business and industry, sometimes even at the managerial level. The climate of war provided the opportunity for more freedom and more access to money, goods and services. Changing cultural norms meant that single women began to enjoy a greater degree of independence. During the 1950s it became socially acceptable for young single women to leave home and to live on their own with other women their own age while working or completing educations, and some young women used their new-found freedom to postpone marriage. The end of the war also brought greater acceptance of women in higher education, and new educational and career opportunities were opened to them. This resulted in a large increase in high school and university attendance on the part of women in eastern Nova Scotia and Cape Breton in the 1950s.

Education for Professional Work

Few Highland Scottish women thought of entering the professions before the 1950s, because few professions were open to them, but a small number of independent and strong-minded women entered careers through teaching and nursing. Single women could only enter these professions on the condition that they would leave when they got married. Some Highland women attributed their love of learning to the traditional music, poetry and folk tales that spurred the mind and the imagination.[22] Others attributed it to a keen desire to better themselves.[23]

Among the earlier generations of Highland Scots the opportunity for schooling was limited to men, but gradually the clergy and the sisters encouraged families to encourage women to get an education. A number of prominent religious and community leaders, including Rev. Thomas Trotter, Bishop John Cameron and Dr. Moses Coady, expressed concern about the neglect of the education of females in eastern Nova Scotia and called for measures to remedy the situation. In the second half of the 19th century, the bishops and priests of the Diocese of Antigonish persuaded the Sisters of Notre Dame and the Sisters of Charity to open convent schools in eastern Nova Scotia. These schools enabled some academically-inclined daughters of the Highland Scots to acquire a high school education. As early as 1852, girls had access to secondary education in Arichat, where the Sisters of Notre Dame opened a convent school.[24]

In the 1880s the Sisters of Notre Dame expanded the opportunities for a high school education for young women by establishing convent schools in Pictou, New Glasgow, Antigonish, Port Hood and Sydney. The most prominent of these schools were St. Bernard's Convent in Antigonish and Holy Angels Convent in Sydney. The quality of the education offered at St. Bernard's was so high that provincial government officials classified it as an academy in 1886.[25] From its very beginning, Holy Angels Convent offered a strong academic program with a focus on the fine arts, and this school did a

Fig. 33 First graduating class from Mt. St. Bernard College, 1897. Photo by: Waldren. St. FX Archives. 89-1480-1570.

great deal to develop a taste for and an appreciation of the fine arts in the greater Sydney area.[26] In 1886, the Sisters of Charity moved into North Sydney and opened Mount St. Joseph Convent to provide an education for girls in that town.[27] St. Bernard's, Holy Angels and Mount St. Joseph established boarding schools to enable girls from the surrounding countryside to go to high school. Through attendance at these schools, girls could obtain the academic background needed to enter the teaching and nursing professions.

St. Bernard's Convent in Antigonish, later known as Mount St. Bernard, brought university education to women in eastern Nova Scotia in 1894 when it began to offer a degree program.[28] The majority of its early graduates were Highland Scots, and many of these women became role models who in turn influenced girls to think about pursuing higher education.

Teaching

In the first few decades of Highland settlement in eastern Nova Scotia and Cape Breton, most children did not go to school. References were made to this problem by provincial government officials in 1825 and again in 1863.[29] The demand for teachers was small, and the jobs were at first reserved for men. It was not until 1838 that the Nova Scotia assembly permitted local school boards to begin hiring women. Married women were not permitted to teach, but if they were widowed they could return to the classroom. In the decades following the introduction of free public schools with the passage of the Free Public School Acts of 1864, 1865 and 1866, women came to outnumber men as teachers. Within forty years of gaining the legal right to teach, women made up two-thirds of the public school teaching force in Nova Scotia.[30] The percentage of women in the teaching profession in Nova Scotia rose from just under 70 per cent in 1871 to over 90 per cent by 1921.[31] Eastern Nova Scotia lagged behind the rest of the province in the feminization of the teaching profession, however. In 1879, 59 per cent of the teaching force in Pictou County was female, as was 40 per cent of the teaching force in both Antigonish and Victoria counties, and 26 per cent in Inverness County.[32]

Formal teacher training became available to women from eastern Nova Scotia in 1854 when the Nova Scotia government opened the Provincial Normal School in Truro to train teachers. In its early years, this institution was a high school offering some coursework in teacher education to prepare its students for teaching careers.[33] Shortly after 1854, the Arichat convent began to incorporate course work in teacher education into its high school program. Sisters of Notre Dame who graduated from this school joined the staff of St. Bernard's Convent School when it opened in Antigonish in 1883.[34] St. Bernard's High School also incorporated some provision for teacher education into its high school program. The interest in teacher education was so great at this school that by 1890, 57 of its high school graduates qualified for teaching licences in the province of Nova Scotia.[35] This school is credited with playing a unique role in the education of the Diocese of Antigonish, because for many years after the closure of the Arichat convent it was the sole supplier of convent-trained teachers.[36] In 1909, the Provincial Normal School in Truro began to require candidates to pass high school examinations as a condition for admission and with this move it achieved recognition as a college.[37]

Older Highland Scottish women who had been teachers remember how poor the remuneration was for them and their predecessors. Until the 1950s, salaries for female teachers were substantially lower than those for men. Agnes MacLellan, a teacher from Linacy, made this comment about the effects of the salary differential: "I remember well how hard it was for a widow with children to get by on this salary." Until 1875, only men could receive the highest licences, levels A and B, making the C license the highest a woman could attain.[38] For decades the trustees of each school district had the authority to determine teachers' salaries and, supported by the licencing rules, they paid lower salaries to women than to men.

In advertisements for teachers, each applicant was asked to state his or her expected salary,[39] which enabled trustees to play one applicant against another, with the job going to the person willing to take the lowest salary. The decline in the percentage of male teachers was related to the abundance of female teachers with the lowest licenses, D and E, and to the tendency of school trustees to hire them because it was cost effective. In 1921, the average salary for female teachers in Nova Scotia was $667 per year compared to more than $1200 per year for men.[40] According to Christena MacDonald from Pleasant Valley, "In the 1930s, the salaries for female teachers were so low that some women left teaching for domestic work in Boston."

The claim that female teachers were performing their natural female nurturing function rather than exercising professional skill was also used to justify the wage differential between female and male teachers.[41] Another common argument for different salaries was the prevailing notion that men as traditional breadwinners needed more money than women. More than 90 per cent of the female teachers were single and lived at home or in boarding houses,[42] and trustees believed that female teachers could live on less money than male teachers. Little consideration was given to the fact that the majority of the female teachers were making equally important financial contributions to their families and that a good number of them came from households headed by a woman.[43] This economic situation was particularly hard on widows. In spite of all these problems, teaching was viewed to be a respectable job for women and provided them with some degree of upward mobility. The financial assistance many female teachers provided for their families made additional education and upward mobility for other family members possible. Many well-educated Highland Scottish men recall the financial sacrifices of female relatives to help them through university.

The history of education from 1808 to 1856 in Nova Scotia is in large measure the story of the struggle for compulsory assessment, tying provision of a free public school system to a fair (and compulsory) tax assessment.[44] Before 1850, most schools were financed by some combination of government grants, tuition from students, private donations and churches.[45] The mechanism for achieving compulsory assessment was put in place in Nova Scotia by the Free School Act of 1864, which placed the schools in each section of each school district under the jurisdiction of a board of

Fig. 34 One-room Morven School, Keppoch. Courtesy Antigonish Heritage Museum. 2006.012.001.

130

Fig. 35 Arisaig schoolchildren and teacher in 1895. Courtesy Antigonish Heritage Museum. 01.80.

three trustees who were given the authority to determine teachers' salaries.[46] The trustees were to obtain the money for teachers' salaries from a local school tax which they were to collect from families in each school section. Compulsory assessment was introduced by the Free School Act of 1865 and refined by its subsequent amendments.[47] This legislation provided the basis for financing public school education until 1942.

The first legislation making attendance compulsory for children aged seven to twelve was passed in 1882 and this further raised the demand for teachers.[48] It also put more pressure on the trustees to raise and collect the school tax. Eastern Nova Scotia was not a prosperous economy in the 19th century, and cash was scarce for Nova Scotia families. Trustees were often unsuccessful in their efforts to collect the education tax. Sr. Sarah MacPherson, who was brought up on a farm in Upper South River, noted: "At that time our families did not have the cash to pay the school tax or any other tax." It was not uncommon for ratepayers to pay a portion of their school tax in the form of farm produce and, accordingly, many teachers received part of their pay in kind.

Poor salaries for teachers were matched by poor working conditions. By the 1920s there were hundreds of one room schools in eastern Nova Scotia, and this situation continued until well into the 1940s, when post-war building booms and the population boom created new opportunities. Highland women who had been teachers recalled that their one room schools lacked central heating and plumbing and that many of them taught all the basic subjects for grades one through ten inclusive.

Fig. 36 School children in Lochaber,-Antigonish County. Courtesy Antigonish Heritage Museum. 2006.025.003.

In 1901, the average age for female teachers was 23; women were discouraged from remaining in teaching after marriage.[49] By 1921 the average age for female teachers had risen to 31 as more remained single to continue their professional careers.[50] This may be partially attributed to the reduced opportunity to marry because of the out-migration of young men and the male death toll in World War I. Some young women, like Agnes MacLellan, taught until they were old enough to gain admission to the Normal College."At the age of seventeen I was not old enough to be admitted to the Normal College, but I was deemed old enough to obtain a temporary permit to get a job teaching all grades from one to ten in a one room school."

There are reports of women as young as fifteen taking teaching positions, many of whom expected to leave teaching once they got married. The stability of the female teaching force that had been achieved in the 1920s was set back by the Depression of the 1930s when poor salaries drove many teachers from the classroom. Salaries dropped so low that often they were not sufficient to cover the teachers' basic needs.

If the young female teacher was not able to live at home, she boarded with a family in the community in which she taught.[51] In either case she found herself living with little privacy and independence. Teachers who returned to the profession as widows often found it difficult to obtain accommodations in the communities in which they were employed. To remedy this, the inspector of schools for Antigonish County recommended the construction of accommodations to house teachers and their families, a practice followed in other eastern counties as well.

The living conditions of female teachers were not nearly as attractive as their social lives. Teachers were considered of superior social status in the communities and a young female teacher was treated as someone special. At school socials and dances, young men vied for the opportunity to dance with them and to escort them home. Margaret MacGregor from Upper South River remembered that: "Young men viewed dating the teacher to be a source of prestige." These young men often had their mothers prepare fine dinners to which they invited the teacher.

Most of the improvements in education from 1926 to 1932 focused on upgrading the teaching profession.[52] In 1927, university teacher training departments were established, and the Nova Scotia Summer School was instituted to upgrade the qualifications of teachers in service. In 1932, all new teachers were required to have a full year of professional education;[53] however, the poor drawing power of the teaching profession, because of low pay, undermined efforts at improvement. In order to staff many rural schools, the trustees found it necessary to continue to hire teachers with lower licences. The reality of the situation was that while the provincial Department of Education was trying to upgrade the qualifications of teachers, many local trustees continued to value teachers with low licences because they were cheap labour and hence less burden to the finances of the school section. The result was that in the 1940s there were still many teachers in rural schools who were teaching without the benefit of any education beyond high school and without any formal teacher training.

By the late 1930s there was ample evidence that financing schools by sections did not work,[54] because ability to pay varied from section to section, as did interest in providing quality education. Additionally, educational authorities recognized the limitations of the one room school and the deplorable state of teacher salaries. Both these problems made securing qualified teachers a serious problem. In 1942, the Nova Scotia government introduced legislation that made the municipal unit responsible for education and placed the financial administration of rural schools in the hands of municipal school boards.[55] The province established an equalization fund to reduce inequities in financing at the municipal level and provide for a minimum salary scale for teachers. In 1946, the provincial government took the progressive step of announcing a new rural high school policy.[56] The province would provide funding to cover the entire capital cost of building a chain of rural high schools throughout the province, and it agreed to share up to 75 per cent of the cost of salaries, maintenance and conveyance for these schools.

In 1953 the Nova Scotia government appointed Vincent Pottier to examine the entire system of educational finance in the province of Nova Scotia and his report proposed a complete reorganization of the public school system.[57] He recommended a partnership of between the municipalities and the province, with municipal governments contributing according to their financial ability and the provincial government paying the balance of the cost of educational needs. The proposal took into account the differences in the financial capabilities of the municipalities. The program was designed to ensure a sufficient number of qualified teachers and adequate school plants, with provision for maintenance and, where necessary, transportation. In 1956, legislation implementing these recommendations came into effect and led to an expansion in school facilities and teaching staff.

The financial rewards for teachers improved markedly as a result of the salary scale of 1956.[58] Improved salaries had the desired effect of bringing a large increase to the number of university graduates entering the profession. For female teachers, changes in licensing and in salary grids meant that for the first time they achieved professional equality with male teachers. They shared with male teachers the joy of working in new modern facilities and they appreciated the marked improvement in teaching loads brought by the consolidation of schools, which made possible the specialization of teaching assignments at the secondary level. These measures encouraged female teachers-in-service to pursue additional education and more women pursued university degrees.

Women also obtained employment in specialized subject areas, particularly at the high school level. While the Normal College continued to produce the majority of new teachers, the number of university-trained teachers, both male and female, increased markedly. Furthermore, increasing numbers of graduates of the Normal College, the majority of whom were female, went on to pursue university degrees on a full-time or part-time basis. Highland Scottish women in large numbers took advantage of these opportunities. Those already in the profession attended Saturday classes, evening classes and summer school to improve their qualifications. The payment of tuition by the province for students enrolled in pre-service teacher education programs enabled bright young women of limited economic means to enter teaching.

During the first half of the 20th century, very few women pursued careers as university teachers; in fact, very few women braved the male-dominated world of graduate studies. A notable exception was Sr. Mairi Macdonald, better known as Mother St. Veronica, a member of the Sisters of Notre Dame. In 1937, she became the first woman appointed to the faculty of St. Francis Xavier University.[59] It seemed fitting that an institution which Highland Scots were instrumental in founding and which served the Highland Scots in eastern Nova Scotia should have as its first female professor a Highland Scot from the area. Sr. Macdonald was a highly respected history professor who is most fondly remembered for her love of Highland Scottish history that she imparted to her students. Her brother, Angus L. Macdonald, was also successful. He was a lawyer who served as the premier of Nova Scotia from 1933 to 1940 and again from 1945 until his death in 1954. With the opening of the doors of St. Francis Xavier University to female teachers, other women soon followed in Sr. Macdonald's footsteps. By the close of the 1950s, the number of

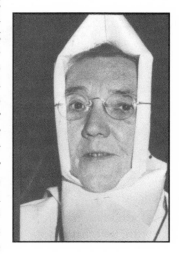

Fig. 37 Sr. Mairi Macdonald, first female faculty member, St. FX University. Courtesy St. FX Archives. 2006-08-15.

female faculty at the university had increased to sixteen, most of whom were sisters.

Nursing

Another career opportunity that opened to Highland Scottish women around the turn of the century was nursing. Nursing schools were established at Aberdeen Hospital, New Glasgow in 1897, at St. Joseph's Hospital, Glace Bay in 1905, and at Hamilton Memorial Hospital, North Sydney in 1911.[60] The Sisters of St. Martha opened nursing schools in most of the hospitals they established in the eastern communities. Nursing sisters held administrative and leadership roles in the hospitals and in the nursing schools run by their congregations. From their ranks came sisters who served as hospital administrators, head nurses and clinical instructors in nursing schools. Some of these nursing sisters also served on the executive of committees of the province's Registered Nurses Association. Some of the young Highland Scottish women who went to New England in the late-19th and early-20th centuries went through nursing school in American hospitals. The sisters and lay women who administered or taught in the early nursing

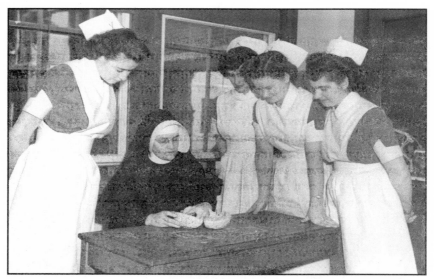

Fig. 38 Instructing nursing students at St. Martha's School of Nursing, Antigonish. Courtesy Archives of the Sisters of St. Martha. 36.

programs in the hospitals in eastern Nova Scotia and Cape Breton obtained their training on the job working with doctors or in nursing programs in the United States or in other parts of Canada.

Young women were drawn into the nursing profession by its orientation toward helping people.[61] Nursing schools and the profession viewed qualities of nurturing and caring to be integral to nursing. Candidates for nursing also tended to view nursing as a source of prestige because of its importance to society.[62]

The early nursing schools in Nova Scotia, as in the rest of Canada, were patterned after the Nightingale system of educating nurses in England.[63] Nursing schools were owned, controlled and operated by the hospitals in which they were located, and it was through service to these hospitals that nurses got their education. In 1962, the Canadian Nurses Association, in its submission to the Royal Commission on Health Services, argued that "many serious weaknesses in nursing education resulted from the control of the school of nursing by an institution whose primary aim was service."[64] As an apprenticeship program, nursing education was secondary to the care of the patients,[65] and there was little emphasis on the theoretical knowledge behind nursing procedures.[66] Even in the middle of the 20th century, nursing instructors lamented that many non-nursing functions were still allocated to nursing service.

Highland women who became nurses have vivid recollections of the domestic work their training program required. Winnie MacEachern, who trained in St. Martha's Hospital in Antigonish, recalled how hard the housekeeping work was: "We washed, waxed and polished the floors in the rooms and hallways of the hospital, cleaned and dusted the furniture and changed the beds." These chores were over and above their responsibility of caring for patients. In spite of their domestic role, the graduates of the early nursing programs reported that as trainees and practising nurses they were treated with respect by both doctors and patients. Mary Ann Chisholm, also a graduate of the nursing program at St. Martha's Hospital, elaborated this view: "The doctors were wonderful to work with. They were our friends. They went out of their way to make us feel important. As for the patients, we found that most of them looked up to us." Positive views of nursing were sometimes contradicted by those who viewed lay nursing as lacking social status because of the domestic work associated with it. Additionally, some of the public was offended by the contact female nurses had with the bodies of their male patients. Usually being a nurse in the armed services was a source of prestige, and the service of nurses in World War I helped to enhance their public image.

The apprenticeship approach to nursing education was partly by necessity. Hospitals had to support themselves from the meager fees they were able to collect from patients, and they put service to the health of even the poorest patients ahead of concern for their ability to pay. Hospital administrators often forgave outstanding debts on compassionate grounds. The check-off system set aside a portion of each miner's salary for health care and provided some hospitals in the industrial areas of Cape Breton with the assurance of a modest payment for service. The services that nursing students provided were important in helping hospitals survive financially by enabling them to keep their complement of higher-paid registered nurses to a minimum. Like teachers, trained nurses were expected to leave hospital work when they married, but many of these women continued to provide service to their communities in one way or another, often on a charitable basis. According to Margaret MacGregor from Upper South River, "A nurse would go to a home where someone was sick or where a mother was about to give birth and stay there until the person she attended was fully recovered. She often received no money for her service." Nurses performed the duties of midwives in their communities, and they usually took care of the mother after the birth of the child.

One of the main arguments against the apprenticeship approach to nursing education was its limited attention to the theory underlying nursing; classroom instruction suffered when the emphasis was on ward duty. While learning on the job had its limitations, it also had the strength of enabling nursing students to benefit from the tutelage of qualified nursing sisters and lay nurses. These mentors served not only as role models for the practice of nursing, but they also exhibited the humane qualities that make health care work a valuable community service.

Until 1910, there were no minimal external requirements for entrance to nursing programs in Nova Scotia; it was up to each hospital to establish its own requirements. Nor were there external controls over hospital nursing programs. Each hospital determined the content of its own nursing program. In 1910, this changed when the provincial government passed legislation entitled An Act to Incorporate the Graduate Nurses Association of Nova Scotia, which authorized the executive committee of the Graduate Nurses Association of Nova Scotia to regulate the study of nursing, preliminary qualifications, length of training and many other matters pertaining to the quality of graduate nurses.[67] In effect, this legislation gave the Registered Nurses Association the authority to regulate the practice of nursing. After its passage, nursing continued through the apprenticeship program, but the nursing programs were now limited to approved schools. Compulsory nursing school examinations were introduced in 1927 in Nova Scotia and became a requirement for registration. By 1931, a grade ten high-school certificate was the minimum requirement for admission to nursing, and by 1936 a Grade 11 certificate was required.

Developments in nursing education in the United States influenced nursing education throughout Canada. The first significant step in establishing standards in the United States came with the publication of *The Standard Curriculum for Schools of Nursing* in 1917, which was widely used in Canada, as were two succeeding versions in 1927 and 1937.[68] In these publications, the nursing profession's view of what constituted an acceptable standard for the preparation of nurses was promulgated. In 1924, these works influenced the Registered Nurses Association of Nova Scotia to establish their own Committee on the Standardization of Training Schools.[69] This committee was responsible for curriculum development and for preparing the examinations students wrote to qualify for registration. During the 1940s, the Committee on the Standardization of Training Schools devoted most of its efforts to building a detailed curriculum for the schools of nursing in the province. The committee specified the subjects taught, the content of these subjects, the textbooks, the number of hours to be devoted to each subject and the bibliography that was to accompany each course. This curriculum was the "bible" for nursing school faculties until the 1960s. In 1955, Nova Scotia introduced the Test Pool Exams, used by the National League of Nurses in New York, as the basis for examining nursing candidates' eligibility for registration.[70]

In 1926, a degree program for nurses was established by St. Francis Xavier University in affiliation with St. Martha's School of Nursing. At that time, the university began a five-year Bachelor

of Science in Nursing program that required that candidates attend university for one year, St. Martha's School of Nursing for the
following three years and then return to university for a fifth and
final year. Few nurses opted to take this program, and the more
common route to nursing was the three-year diploma program.
Many young women from the Highland Scottish communities in
eastern Nova Scotia were able to attend nursing school because
the hospital schools did not charge tuition.

During World War II, the position of clinical instructor was
developed in response to a depletion in the ranks of head nurses
through their recruitment to war service.[71] Head nurses who remained at home now had to assume the responsibilities of those
who joined the forces, and this meant that head nurses could no
longer afford time for teaching service. To fill this gap, the position
of clinical instructor was born. Despite considerable opposition
from those in nursing education who viewed this position as further separating theory and practice, the position became firmly
established.

Some women entered military service as nurses to do work
that was viewed as exciting and prestigious. One outstanding
example of such a nurse was Major
Margaret MacDonald, a Highland
Scot from Bailey's Brook in Pictou
County who had a remarkable nursing career in the military service.[72] In
1895, she graduated in nursing from
the Charity Hospital Training School
in New York. Three years later, she
was off to the Boer War, one of five
young Canadian women selected
from hundreds of applicants for
the Canadian Army Medical Corps.
She then went to Panama during
the construction of the Canal to
nurse men sick with yellow fever
and malaria. When she returned,
she was appointed Lieutenant in the
permanent force of the Canadian
Army Medical Corps and she sailed
with the first contingent of Canadian

Fig. 39 Major Margaret C.
MacDonald, head of the Allied
Nursing Corps, World War I,
1915. The MacDonald family
collection. Courtesy St. FX
Archives. MG78.

troops in World War I. Under her leadership, the nursing corps was organized and directed from her headquarters in London, England. In her leadership capacity she travelled across the Western Front planning, organizing and inspecting nursing services. For her achievements, King George V conferred on her the Decoration of the Royal Red Cross, and following the ceremony she was invited to dine privately with the King and Queen. Her obituary eloquently celebrated her achievements:

> From that fledgling class of fifty-three years ago one was destined to dine with royalty, to know prelates and generals; to be honoured by society for an errand of mercy that took her through pestilence and war in three continents; in the annals of the noblest of Canadian womanhood her name is written large and honorably.[73]

Nine

Women in Religious Congregations

Three religious congregations served the Highland Scottish families of eastern Nova Scotia and Cape Breton: the Sisters of Notre Dame, the Sisters of Charity and the Sisters of St. Martha. Services provided by each congregation fall into the general categories of education, health and social welfare and were sufficiently different to enable them to complement and supplement one another in their efforts to improve the quality of life of the Highland Scots in eastern Nova Scotia.

The religious atmosphere in Highland Catholic homes encouraged young women to take up religious vocations, further nourished through contact with sisters in convent schools. One of these women, Sr. Peggy MacFarlane from Margaree, reported that "these sisters were an integral part of life in our community, and their lives touched the lives of many people. They had a tremendous influence on us." Teaching sisters were role models for young women, who observed first hand the good work the sisters did in the schools, churches and communities. Sr. Peggy MacFarlane noted the spiritual element of their work. "In the final analysis," she stated, "a religious vocation is a calling, something that comes from within." The lives of the sisters were devoted to nurturing spirituality in themselves through daily participation in the mass, prayer, meditation and spiritual reading and service to others.

The Sisters of Notre Dame

The Congregation de Notre Dame (CND) was founded by Marguerite Bourgeois when she opened her first school in Montreal in 1658.[1] The Order served in early 18th-century Louisbourg and it was the first congregation of sisters to serve the Highland Scots of eastern Nova Scotia. These sisters were primarily a teaching order, and it was through teaching in their schools in Pictou, Antigonish, Inverness and Cape Breton counties that they influenced the lives of countless young women. Their major convents were also boarding schools which drew young women from all over the region. In the early years of their mission in eastern Nova Scotia, the sisters gave many young women access to a high school education which would not otherwise have been available to them.

The order's founder, Marguerite Bourgeois, held that "education is the development of the whole child, body, intellect and will under the four-fold aspects of the religious, the aesthetic, the domestic and the economic."[2] This philosophy of education provided direction for the programs offered in the CND convent schools and for the way of life of their students. In these schools the requirements of the Board of Education for the province of Nova Scotia were supplemented by instruction in religion, the practical arts of home-making and the fine arts (music, art and drama). Their students staged public performances which brought the arts to the community. Marguerite Bourgeois's emphasis on the household skills of sewing and weaving was applied in the convent schools through the development of courses in domestic science. The tradition of teaching household arts was so strong at Mount St. Bernard that in 1917 its domestic science program was approved as a training program for teachers.[3]

The work of the sisters of Notre Dame in Nova Scotia began before the arrival of the Highland Scots. They taught young French women in Louisbourg from 1732 to 1758, with two interruptions during military activities.[4] Because their accomplishments at Louisbourg were so successful, Bishop Colin Francis MacKinnon, the second Bishop of Arichat, requested the sisters to return to Cape Breton in 1857, this time to Arichat. There they established a convent boarding school which served as a model for some of the other schools they established later in Nova Scotia.

The first convent school they established on the mainland of eastern Nova Scotia was Stella Maris in Pictou, which opened in 1880.[5] The sisters came to Pictou at the urging of the parish priest, Fr. Ronald MacDonald, and they helped him raise $1,800 for a new convent by organizing a three-day bazaar in September 1880. The sisters continued to contribute to the support of the school by holding bazaars and student concerts. The school offered a business program in clerical and secretarial work that prepared the young women of Pictou County to take advantage of new employment opportunities. The sisters also established St. John's Academy in New Glasgow, which opened in 1887,[6] and the parish financed the construction and maintenance of the school and the convent.

After the seat of the diocese was moved from Arichat to Antigonish in 1882, one of Bishop John Cameron's aspirations was to establish a convent school in Antigonish where girls could enjoy the same educational and cultural opportunities as boys.[7] This convent was described as the "lineal descendent of the Arichat Convent."[8] Bishop Cameron's initiative resulted in the opening of St. Bernard's Convent and School in 1883, later known as Mount St. Bernard.[9] Many of the teachers had been educated at the Arichat convent. In its first year of operation the convent school had 86 day pupils and four residents; toward the close of the decade the number of students in residence ranged between forty and fifty, the great majority of whom were Highland Scots from Antigonish, Pictou and Cape Breton.[10] A small number of Presbyterian girls attended the school, and Betty Ballantyne, a Scottish Presbyterian from Ballantyne's Cove, told the story of "how her mother was so anxious to have her daughter attend the convent school that she approached the superior of the convent to request that she accept butter as payment for her daughter's tuition. Her request was granted."

The sisters offered a common school program for girls covering grades one to eight and added courses to the core program to reflect the sisters' vision of education. In 1884, when the Inspector of Schools first visited the convent school, he was pleased with the quality of education and stated in his annual report: "These highly accomplished ladies hold provincial licenses, and have the reputation of being excellent teachers of the branches taught in our common schools, as well as of music, painting, drawing, and all branches that constitute a thorough female education."[11] An

Fig. 40 Students at Mount St. Bernard Academy, early 1900s. Courtesy Antigonish Heritage Museum. 99.61.71.

Fig. 41 Day students at Mount St. Bernard Academy, 1910. Courtesy Antigonish Heritage Museum. 91.85.

inspection in 1886 resulted in a second glowing report of the work of the teaching sisters: "The excellent character of the work done is well known—a thorough training, polished education, and gentle manners distinguished its graduates."[12] The Inspector of Schools announced that Antigonish had one of the best schools in the province: "Never in my long experience have I examined a class showing such promise and general proficiency."[13] His positive assessment enabled the convent school to qualify for government subsidies as an academy, and the sisters began teaching grades nine through twelve.

In 1886 the school was expanded into three divisions—elementary, intermediate and senior—and it offered broad subject matter ranging from Christian doctrine, reading and writing, to languages, physics, chemistry and teacher training. Some of the science classes were taught by members of the faculty of St. Francis Xavier College. Sr. Mary E. Campbell, a high-school teacher at Mount St. Bernard Academy in the 1950's, recalled that in addition to moulding character in the Christian faith, "we focused on the development of the whole person" with emphasis on politeness, thoughtfulness, consideration for others and self-denial. Prizes were offered not only for academic achievement, but also for religion, social virtues and good conduct.[14] Mount St. Bernard continued to function as an all-girls school for the town of Antigonish until the 1950s when its secondary students transferred to the newly constructed Antigonish High School and its elementary students transferred to Morrison School.

In the late 1880s, both the sisters and the students expressed interest in higher education, but St. Francis Xavier College, located nearby, did not accept female students. When the question of higher education for girls was put to Bishop Cameron, he replied: "If the girls are willing to do the work, why should they not have the same advantages as their brothers";[15] with his approval steps were taken to start a college at St. Bernard's Convent. A number of measures were taken that led to St. Bernard's affiliation with St. Francis Xavier College in 1894,[16] through which it could offer a liberal arts program leading to a baccalaureate degree. In 1897, four of its graduates qualified for degrees. *The Casket* noted that: "For the first time, as far as we know, in the history of Catholic education in America, the degree of Bachelor of Arts is to be conferred on a class of young ladies by a Catholic college."[17] The graduation exercises for female students remained separate from those of St. Francis Xavier College until 1928.[18]

Even though women began to attend classes at St. Francis Xavier College in the 1920s, Mount St. Bernard continued to offer liberal arts courses for first-year students. Secretarial arts were available even before the turn of the century, and a complete secretarial program was established in the 1920s. Approval for a Bachelor of Science program in Home Economics was obtained from the Board of Governors of St. Francis Xavier University in the 1927-1928 academic year. Mount St. Bernard developed courses in art and music in the 1950s, which were open to all students of St. Francis Xavier University.

In the early years of the college, the sisters emphasized the importance of developing cultivated individuals: "This was an age of refinement and culture, an age when education meant nothing if it failed to bear the earmarks of excellence in fine speech and the social graces."[19] The graduates of this well-rounded education had a refining influence on the communities in which they lived.[20] Families of the early graduates reported that their mothers supplemented the education they received in their local schools. Jean MacDonald, of Malignant Cove, testified to the importance of this instruction:

> The quality of instruction the children in our family received in the rural school we attended was poor. Our teachers only had permissive licences. Some of them didn't know much more than we did. My mother was a graduate of St. Bernard's Academy, and she put her education to good use by teaching us at home. We gathered around the kitchen table every night after supper to be instructed in mathematics, English and other subjects. Her teaching gave us a strong background in these subjects and without her help members of our family would not have had the education needed to go into teaching or to attend university.

In the late 1800s, the Sisters of Notre Dame expanded their services to communities in rural and industrial Cape Breton. In Inverness County they established convent schools in Port Hood and Mabou, and opened convents in Iona and in the town of Inverness, where they taught in local parish schools. The sisters brought the same combination of academic subjects, religious education and refined manners and etiquette that reflected their teaching mission.[21] The sisters were sensitive to the material needs as well as the spiritual and educational needs of their students and they often fed and clothed poor and hungry children. When children got wet on the way to school, they dried their clothes. They consoled people in times of sickness and distress. They prepared the children for first communion and confirmation. Through their many services they became an integral part of the life of their communities and: "Two by two they came to visit our homes, the sick and aged in particular, and to pray in our homes," their students recalled.[22] Over and above their teaching duties, the sisters became active in the life of the community.

Parishioners in Mabou requested that the sisters open a convent school, and in 1887 two sisters set up a young ladies academy and boarding school.[23] The people of Mabou helped the sisters keep the convent going through their many donations of food, wood and coal.[24] The opening of the boarding school was followed by the opening of a day school for girls and its success attracted boarders from across rural Cape Breton and eastern mainland. Some families moved to the area so that their daughters could benefit from a convent education.

Word of the good education the sisters at Mabou provided spread to the town of Inverness where, in 1904, in response to public demand the sisters opened Holy Family Convent and taught in the local parish school. As was the case in the other two schools in Inverness County, it was only with the generosity of the parishioners that the sisters were able to keep the school going, and were rewarded for their efforts; in 1905, the pupils were examined in nearly all branches of study, and in each they were found to be remarkably proficient.[25] In 1938, the parish priest and the parishioners of Iona convinced the sisters to establish a convent in their community so that they could become part of the teaching staff of the local school.

The Sisters of Notre Dame ventured into industrial Cape Breton to establish Holy Angels Convent in Sydney in 1885 at the request of the parishioners of the Sacred Heart Parish and their pastor, Fr. James Quinan.[26] It was their hope that a convent boarding school would provide girls with the same quality of education as that available to boys at Sydney Academy. The original convent was paid for by the parishioners of Sydney, Lingan, Low Point and other areas. By 1897, the convent school had six boarders, 94 day students and 30 music pupils for the study of piano, violin, mandolin and guitar. By 1901, the school had registered 200 pupils in six departments. Its boarding school gave young women from the industrial area and the surrounding rural communities access to a high-school education and remained opened until 1936.

The Sydney school became known for the attainments of its pupils in music, drama and art, and from its very beginning the school held choral and instrumental performances to help defray expenses.[27] Closing exercises always included a fine program of vocal and instrumental music, and awards were given for music and drawing excellence. The sisters also prepared some of their pupils to teach music and drawing outside the Sydney area.

The sisters expanded their services in industrial Cape Breton in the early 1900s by opening schools in several other industrial towns.[28] These schools differed from their previous ventures in that the school populations were larger and included boys as well as girls. In 1900, three sisters arrived in Sydney Mines where they established Notre Dame Convent and a convent school—the first school established by the Sisters of Notre Dame to offer classes to boys. In 1902, they opened a school in Holy Redeemer parish in Whitney Pier and, in 1938, with the growth of the steel plant and the influx of workers, its enrolment expanded to more than 1,000 pupils. In 1913, three sisters left Holy Angels Convent to establish St. Agnes Convent and School in New Waterford. In 1941, the sisters assumed teaching duties in New Victoria and taught all grades, and in 1955 they extended their services to a school in St. Theresa's Parish in Sydney.

In addition to their influence on the education of the Highland Scottish women of eastern Nova Scotia and Cape Breton, the Sisters of Notre Dame made a significant contribution to the perpetuation of the Highland Scottish folk culture. Two of the most notable contributors were Sr. Mairi Macdonald and Sr. Margaret Beaton. Sr. Macdonald contributed to the perpetuation of the Gaelic language and Scottish music in 1946 by starting the Mount St. Bernard Gaelic choir comprised of female university students. According to her contemporary and friend, Sr. Margaret MacDonnell, "The choir was the medium through which she hoped to convey to her audiences the urgency of preserving the language as well as the infinite literary and musical treasures to which its preservation would ensure access."[29] Sr. Macdonald cherished efforts of the Highland Scots to set their life experiences to music, and she promoted the gift of expression this music gave them. Her choir performed at many notable events in eastern Canada and made two records of Gaelic and Scottish songs. Her devotion to the perpetuation of the Highland Scottish folk culture had a considerable impact on the decision of St. Francis Xavier University to establish a Department of Celtic Studies in 1958.

Sr. Margaret Beaton's efforts to preserve the Highland Scottish folk culture began with the teaching of Gaelic classes at Xavier Junior College in Sydney in the 1950s. Over the years she developed a passion for collecting primary and secondary source material pertaining to the Highland Scots,[30] and this collection laid the groundwork for the establishment of a centre for the preservation of these documents, named in her honor, the Beaton Institute. Sr. Beaton's collection has grown to become the main archives of Cape Breton.

The Sisters of Charity

The Sisters of Charity, an American congregation founded in 1809 by Sister Elizabeth Ann Seaton in Emmetsburg, Maryland, first extended their services to Nova Scotia in 1849. At the request of Bishop William Walsh of the Diocese of Halifax, they established a mission in Halifax which had a three-fold purpose: educate the young, visit the sick and assist the poor.[31] The Halifax community of the Sisters of Charity became an independent congregation in 1856[32] and extended its services to the Diocese of Antigonish in 1882 during the tenure of Bishop John Cameron. Education was their primary service to eastern Nova Scotia, but they were also involved in health care and social services.

The sisters first worked in Stellarton, where the parish provided an old church building for their first school, but the classrooms were so cold that on many winter mornings the ink was frozen in the inkwells.[33] In 1883, a new convent was completed in Our Lady of Lourdes Parish, and it included improved classroom facilities. Through the influence of Sir John Thompson, the federal government opened a post office in this convent to provide a source of revenue for the school,[34] and this income was augmented by small fees charged to the parents of the pupils, fundraising and personal donations from the pastor.

To educate children from grades one to four, Fr. A. A. Butts built St. Brigid's School in Stellarton in 1919, and the sisters took charge of its operation.[35] One of the teaching sisters wrote that when the school opened, the two teachers found themselves faced with one hundred pupils in grades one to four in classrooms that had no desks or blackboards.[36] School began in September, but the desks and the blackboards did not arrive until December. Until then the children knelt on the hardwood floor and used the seats of the chairs for desks. The school was heated by a pot-bellied stove which not only provided heat, but also a surface for warming and sometimes cooking food for the children's lunches. Despite their limited resources, the sisters provided a solid academic education for their pupils.

In a submission made to the Stellarton School Board in 1922 to obtain financial support, parents claimed that the distinctiveness of parochial schools lies in the importance they attach to religious education. They argued: "The moral training of the child is the most essential part of education; you cannot separate religion from morality nor, therefore, separate religion from education."[37] In addition to teaching religious and academic subjects, the sisters gave their students a taste for the fine arts and coached students to take part in music and speech festivals in New Glasgow. The artistic talents of the pupils were also displayed at annual Christmas concerts and plays.

In 1912, the sisters in Pictou opened a sanatorium in Lourdes for the care of tubercular patients and chronic invalids.[38] During the Spanish flu epidemic of 1918, the sisters who staffed the sanatorium ignored the dangers of this contagious virus and went from home to home to care for stricken families. When necessary, they used the sanatorium as an emergency hospital. The sisters also did social work in Lourdes by dividing the parish into six districts and visiting one each day. The parishioners so admired the sisters for their good works that many families named their newborn daughter after a favourite sister.

The services of the Sisters of Charity were extended to industrial Cape Breton in 1883 and were concentrated primarily in the towns of North Sydney and Glace Bay with satellite missions in Reserve Mines and New Waterford. At the request of Fr. D. J. MacIntosh, the rector of St. Joseph's parish in North Sydney, their Mother General sent four sisters to his parish.[39] Shortly after their arrival, a new convent, Mount St. Joseph, was constructed. In their first seven years in North Sydney these sisters sponsored concerts and other entertainment from which they raised $12,000 that was used to establish a boarding school for girls from the surrounding countryside. In 1907, the resourceful sisters erected an elementary school, in 1913 they built a junior high school and, in 1925, a senior high school.

In 1908, A. G. Hamilton financed the construction of a new hospital in North Sydney and asked the sisters to run it. Sr. Austin, who had been the head nurse at the Halifax Infirmary, was appointed administrator and under her auspices the hospital flourished.[40] Unlike the mining towns where the miners' check-off for health services financed the hospitals, Hamilton Memorial had no reliable source of funds but, through frugality and assistance from the community, the sisters managed to keep the hospital operating.

The nursing sisters lived and worked in the hospital. Seven of these sisters who are now retired came together to reminisce on their experiences. These are some of their recollections:

> The life of a nursing sister was nursing, and it was a life of service to God. I not only worked in the hospital; I lived in the hospital. In the course of my duties I put special emphasis on the spiritual needs of the sick.

Fig. 42 First communion group instructed by a Sister of Charity, Port Hawkesbury. Courtesy Sisters of Charity Congregational Archives. 1066A.

As I look back, I don't know how we managed to do what we did. Each day I got up, went to mass, put in a twelve-hour day on the floors of the hospital, said my prayers and fell into bed. I worked seven days a week. On top of that, I often had to get up at night to attend to emergencies. Our greatest privation was sleep.

I remember what it was like to maintain all-night vigils with patients who were dying. The sisters wanted to make sure that no one died alone. I sat with them, held their hands and prayed with them. I did everything I could not only to comfort the patient but to console the family. That often helped families to come to terms with the death of their loved ones.

There were times when I faced night duty with considerable trepidation. It was a big responsibility. There were no doctors on duty at night, but one of them was always on call. When an emergency required me to call a doctor and wake him out of a sound sleep, I had to convince him that the situation was serious enough to require him to come to the hospital. That was not always easy. Dealing with distraught family members who accompanied emergency cases or with patients who were violent was particularly stressful. I have memories of violent patients who struck fear into my heart. Fortunately, they were few in number.

Fig. 43 Students on stage at St. Theresa's School, Port Hawkesbury. Courtesy Sisters of Charity Congregational Archives. 1066B.

My work and that of the other sisters sometimes extended beyond the bounds of the hospital. When I noticed that my patients were particularly poor, I tried to reach out to them. The nursing sisters did not have time to visit their homes and the teaching sisters did that on our behalf. They often took food and clothing to their homes. Sometimes children found these visits so comforting that they began to find their way to the door of the convent. The sisters made sure that they were welcomed and put them at the table to be fed.

I know our stories of our hospital work make it sound very onerous, but I want to point out that it was also a great source of personal satisfaction. Our chief reward was in knowing that we were helping others. I was often very moved by the heart-felt appreciation of our services expressed by patients and their families.

In 1937, the parish priest and members of the Ladies Auxiliary wrote to a sister who was departing from the Hamilton Memorial Hospital:

We know the tender care, the capable solicitude and loving kindness with which you watched over the numberless patients entrusted to your care during your twenty-six years of service. In joy and in sorrow, in weariness and exaltation, you have ever preserved the calm demeanor and helpful courage possible only to one whose life is that of sacrifice, of service to her fellow creatures.[41]

In 1911 the sisters established a school of nursing in Hamilton Memorial Hospital. The nursing sisters were active in nursing education at the provincial level and were well-represented in the Registered Nurses Association for the province of Nova Scotia. The Hamilton was twice enlarged, but its facilities were never sufficient to meet demands and it was replaced with the new St. Elizabeth's Hospital in 1954 and granted full accreditation.[42] The school of nursing continued in the new hospital and the old hospital was converted into a residence for seniors.

Former nursing sisters at the Hamilton Memorial Hospital who observed the operation of the nursing school described its nursing education program:

The philosophy that guided the work of the nursing sisters carried over into the training offered in the nursing school. The nursing students were encouraged to care for the whole patient, for their spiritual and social needs, as well as their physical needs.

The nursing school was a tremendous service to the hospital because the student nurses augmented the work of the nursing sisters. In addition to their classes, the student nurses worked an eight-hour day on the hospital floors with the nursing sisters and benefited from their experience and close supervision. Participation in religious activities was an integral part of the lives of the student nurses.

Fig. 44 Pharmacy, St. Elizabeth's Hospital, North Sydney. Courtesy Sisters of Charity Congregational Archives. 982A.

In 1894, the sisters opened a convent and school in St. Anne's Parish in Glace Bay,[43] and from here the sisters travelled by wagon or sleigh, depending on the season, to teach in the satellite missions of New Aberdeen, St. Anthony, Passchendale and Caledonia until they were able to establish convents in these areas. All of these schools incorporated religious study, academic subjects and instruction in art, music, drama and elocution.[44] The sisters had a hard time coping with the increase in enrolment that resulted from the influx of people working in the mines. By 1936, enrolment in these schools grew to 1,300 pupils.

In addition to their teaching duties, the sisters helped with the liturgy, missions and entertainment; they prepared the children for first communion and confirmation; and they established sodalities, organizations devoted to fostering religious devotion and to carrying out good works. During the Depression of the 1930s, their resources were stretched to provide food and clothing for the poor, and many in the industrial area had high praise for the work the sisters did for those in need.

At the invitation of the parish priest of Reserve Mines, Fr. Roderick MacInnis, the sisters moved into St. Joseph's Parish where they opened an elementary school and a high school in 1903.[45] When Fr. Jimmy Tompkins became pastor in 1935, he persuaded the sisters to expand their educational mission to include adult education.[46] He asked for the services of Sr. Frances Dolores Donnelly, a trained librarian, to assist in establishing and operating a "People's Library" in Reserve Mines. Sr. Donnelly stated that "miners who had limited education, who had never read before, became regular customers."[47] Cynics predicted that the books would be stolen or ruined, but both children and parents took good care of the books and returned them to the library.

Fig. 45 St. Anne's Convent, Glace Bay, opened 1893. Courtesy Sisters of Charity Congregational Archives. 856.

This was the first school library in the province of Nova Scotia to be organized by a professional librarian and supported by school-board funds. It laid the basis for a regional library system that was legislated in 1948 to serve the entire province.[48] Sr. Donnelly believed that: "Libraries are the door to a better life for all, but particularly for that broad group of people who have only basic education."[49] Fr. Tompkins said of Donnelly that she was "one of the most gifted and effective of his associates in adult education" in her ability to bring library services to the people.[50] She shared Tompkins's view that libraries would become "the universities" of the people.

When the Sisters of Notre Dame withdrew from New Waterford in 1921, the Sisters of Charity took over their parish schools at Mt. Carmel and St. Agnes.[51] In their contacts with the school children the sisters quickly became aware of the social and economic problems of the community. To provide assistance to the people of the parish, they established a social service center in the basement of the convent to help the poor and the needy.

In 1891, at the invitation of Fr. Alexander Beaton, the Sisters of Charity opened a convent school in Havre Boucher in a three-room school provided by the parish.[52] The people of this small rural parish welcomed the sisters with generous supplies of food, bed linens, blankets, cutlery, utensils and other necessities. The good work of the sisters in Havre Boucher prompted Fr. Angus Beaton to request they open a school in St. Mary's Parish, Port Hawkesbury. This school served pupils from grades one to eleven for forty years. In addition to their teaching services, the sisters taught catechism, directed the choir, instructed converts and visited the sick and poor.

Fig. 46 Sr. Frances Dolores Donnelly, pioneer of the Regional Library system for Nova Scotia. Photo by: Horvath, Eaton's photography. Sisters of Charity Congregational Archives. 1914B.

The Sisters of Charity have fond memories of their years in the classrooms of eastern Nova Scotia.[53] They became very close to the pupils and their parents and learned a great deal about the communities in which they taught, through home visitations. Sr. Johanna Hogan, retired after many years of teaching in Glace Bay, recounts her personal view of the relationship between the teaching sisters and the community:

> We became an integral part of the communities in which we taught. Every evening after supper some of the sisters visited homes in the community. We took baskets of food to people in need. We visited patients in the hospital. When there was a death in a family, we went to the home to console the relatives. We appreciated the warmth of the welcome the people extended to us. I think our interest in the community made us more sensitive to the problems our pupils faced.
>
> Sometimes the harsh side of life in the mining communities touched our schools. I shall never forget the day the father of a dear little boy in my class was killed in the mine while school was in session. Our efforts to console the distraught boy reduced us all to tears.

The sisters encouraged and assisted female students to enter nursing school. When they sensed that young women had a religious vocation, they helped them to learn more about that path in life. They encouraged young women to go to Normal College or to university, and in some cases they helped them to get financial aid for their tuition.

The structural reorganization of the school system that followed World War II and the changes brought by the implementation of the recommendations of the Pottier Commission Report in 1956 had a tremendous effect on the teaching services of the Sisters of Charity. These changes resulted in the building of large, modern schools which, over a period of time, replaced the schools that had been built and operated by the Sisters of Charity. Most of the teaching sisters moved from their own schools to teach in the local public schools.[54] With these changes the sisters saw the need to begin conceptualizing new ways of serving the people.

The Sisters of Saint Martha

The congregation of the Sisters of St. Martha was founded by Bishop John Cameron of the Diocese of Antigonish to provide domestic service for St. Francis Xavier College.[55] Between 1894 and 1900, a total of thirty-one women from the Diocese of Antigonish went to Halifax to receive domestic training as postulants in the auxiliary order of the Sisters of Charity.[56] The postulants learned household management in addition to induction into religious life that included prayer, meditation, spiritual reading and instruction in Christian doctrine and religious vows. At the end of their novitiate, the sisters returned to St. Francis Xavier College to establish the convent that remained a mission of the Sisters of Charity until 1900. At that time, the convent at St. Francis Xavier College became the motherhouse of the Sisters of St. Martha, and it was there that the sisters had their first novitiate. The sisters worked under the jurisdiction of the priests who administered the university, and in the early decades of this order Highland women from eastern Nova Scotia were the most highly represented group.[57]

The duties of the sisters at the college included cooking and housekeeping for the priests and the all-male student population. In its early years, the university had a farm called Mount Cameron that produced vegetables, fruit, milk and meat. The sisters who first staffed the kitchen at the university carried cans of milk to the basement to be put on ice and hauled bags of potatoes and turnips and carcasses of beef that parents brought to the campus as payment in kind for their children's tuition.[58] Eventually, men were hired by the university to take over these tasks.

In their serving roles, the sisters nursed and mothered the students and brought a home-like atmosphere to residential life at the college. Many graduates remember fondly the lengths to which the sisters went to prepare great quantities of home-cooked food that the students liked, including home-made breads and biscuits served fresh from the oven.[59] The sisters' spiritual influence helped to deepen the faith of students, and their domestic service gave them many opportunities to listen to and provide counsel for the young men who honoured the sisters by calling them "our mothers away from home."[60]

With the approval of college administrators, in 1906, the sisters opened a cottage hospital on St. Ninian's Street in Antigonish

Fig. 47 Original motherhouse of the Sisters of St. Martha, to the right of Xavier Hall. Courtesy Antigonish Heritage Museum. 00.64.41.

town with six beds, an operating room and a kitchen.[61] From this humble beginning, hospital service grew in Antigonish until, in 1926, increased demand led to the construction of a new modern hospital. In connection with this hospital, a fifty-bed sanatorium for the care of tuberculosis patients was erected by the provincial government in 1933.

For nearly a century, preparation for nursing had been an apprenticeship program in which students learned to nurse by nursing, and this is the way it was in the early years of the nursing program at St. Martha's Hospital.[62] In 1911, the sisters opened a school of nursing there, offering a three-year diploma program.[63] Students received nursing education in exchange for their service to the hospital. The nursing education program emphasized the spiritual as well as the physical care of the sick. This program became more professional over time with the addition of formal courses in nursing and organized clinical experiences. In 1926, the professional dimension of nursing was furthered when St. Martha's School of Nursing affiliated with St. Francis Xavier University to offer a Bachelor of Science degree in nursing.

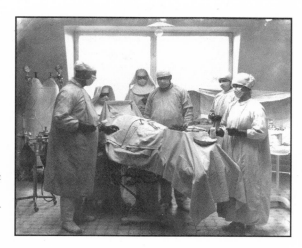

Fig. 48 Sisters assisting in the operating room at St. Martha's Hospital, 1930s. Courtesy Archives of the Sisters of St. Martha. 17.

As the congregation expanded and flourished, the sisters came to view their dependence on the college as a constraint and this became a source of dissatisfaction. They felt the time had come to end the control of the College Council of Priests over them and, on August 4, 1917, that very council agreed that the sisters could direct their own organization, subject to the bishop of the diocese. At the same time, they were to continue their domestic service at the university.64 With this change the sisters gained input into determining the direction of their mission and greater control over their destiny. They expanded their services from domestic work into social welfare and teaching, and they extended their health care services. Their work was usually initiated in response to requests from the bishop, priests and lay people of the diocese, but

Fig. 49 The cottage hospital, Antigonish, which moved to Harris House in 1907. Courtesy Antigonish Heritage Museum. 2003.141.001.

the sisters now had more say in how this work was planned and conducted. In 1921, as a mark of their independence, the sisters constructed a new motherhouse, away from the grounds of the university, known to this day as Bethany.

Until 1902, there were no hospitals in the Diocese of Antigonish.[65] St. Joseph's Hospital in Glace Bay was the first institution of its kind, and Saint Francis Xavier College made the services of five sisters available to take over its domestic service. Two sisters enrolled in its school of nursing that opened at the same time to train nurses to staff the hospital. The hospital was supported by donations from the general public, the Dominion Coal Company and the "check-off," a form of hospital insurance whereby miners paid twenty cents per month to obtain care in a hospital ward.[66]

The hospital was opened because of the frequency of accidents in the mines surrounding Glace Bay and the difficulties of trying to treat seriously injured miners at home. Mary MacNeil from Glace Bay remembered her father describing how "a doctor operated on a family member on their kitchen table." Despite the great need, the sisters withdrew their services from the hospital in 1908 because of internal administrative difficulties. In 1915 the Board of Trustees of the hospital persuaded the sisters to return and to take over the administration of the hospital. The sisters quickly learned the ropes of hospital management, and in 1921 it was accredited by the American College of Surgeons, one of the first hospitals in Canada to be so recognized.[67]

The sisters lived in the hospital and served in every capacity except that of medical doctor. In addition to their professional, clerical and administrative services, they operated the kitchen and the laundry and did all of the domestic work. The sisters who served as administrators attempted to obtain well-qualified medical staff and up-to-date equipment. Evidence of the fine job the sisters did in running the hospital came in 1942 when the hospital was honoured again, this time by the American College of Physicians who determined that St. Joseph's Hospital was one of the most up-to-date hospitals in Canada.[68] The sisters ran St. Joseph's Hospital until it was taken over by the government after a ruling of the Nova Scotia Hospital Insurance Commission in 1959.

The Sisters of St. Martha had long aspired to found a model hospital in Sydney, and in 1920 their ambition was realized when they acquired Ross Memorial Hospital, a convalescent hospital for World War I veterans. After the veterans were transferred to Camp Hill Hospital, the sisters took over the facility, and it became known as St. Rita Hospital.[69] In 1927, the hospital started a nursing school and in 1944 started a training program in x-ray technology. Additions and renovations to the original building were unable to keep pace with the increasing demand for hospital services in the growing city and surrounding rural areas, and in 1951 a new hospital was constructed.

In the early 1920s, the people of Inverness town and county worked together to promote the building of a new hospital and to raise funds for its construction.[70] The greatest contribution to the building campaign came from the coal miners who agreed to have one dollar deducted from each pay cheque for this cause. When the building, which became known as Saint Mary's Hospital, was completed in 1925, the curate of the parish of Inverness, Fr. J. B. Kyte, asked the Sisters of St. Martha to take it over. The services of the sisters and the finances of the hospital were pressed to the limit by the heavy demands of the miners for medical services to treat injuries and accidents, and by the health problems arising from working in the mines. With the beginning of the Depression shortly after the hospital opened, and with the resulting downturn in the mining industry, the financial situation of the hospital deteriorated. To keep the hospital going, the sisters had to forego needed repairs and improvements so that their meager funds could be devoted to patient care. Retired nursing sisters recall how they cut up old bed sheets for bandages in order to save money.[71]

To improve the quality of the care their hospitals provided, the Congregation of the Sisters of St. Martha sent highly competent sisters to some of the best universities in Canada and the United States for advanced study in fields related to hospital work. From their ranks came administrators for their hospitals, supervisors for their nursing services and teachers for their schools of nursing. In 1940, Sr. Mary of Calvary, who for many years was head of the St. Martha's Hospital School of Nursing in Antigonish, became the first nurse in Nova Scotia to obtain a Master's degree in Nursing Education.[72]

One of the outstanding leaders of the order in the provision of health care was Mother Ignatius.[73] In 1910, she entered the congregation, graduated from St. Martha's School of Nursing in 1916, and did four months additional training at St. Michael's Hospital in Toronto. She started her career as director of nurses in St. Joseph's Hospital in Glace Bay, and in 1919 became superintendent of that hospital. In 1925, she became the first Superior General and Mother General of the congregation, serving in that capacity for thirty years. Under her guidance the hospital services provided by the order to the Diocese of Antigonish expanded and flourished.[74] When she started her first term as head of the congregation, it had eight missions and 106 sisters. On the completion of her fifth term, the congregation had 33 missions and 438 sisters.

Mother Ignatius was a principal organizer of the Maritime Conference of the Catholic Hospital Association in 1922, of the Maritime Hospital Association in 1929 and of the Blue Cross Insurance plan in 1942. She served for eight years on the Canadian Hospital Council and in 1956 was granted the Stephens Award for outstanding contribution to hospital work, stating that: "She was the first woman, the first member of a religious order, and the first person from the Maritimes to receive this honor."[75] In 1957, recognition of her outstanding contribution to hospital administration led to her appointment to the Hospital Services Planning Commission established by the Government of Nova Scotia to formulate plans for a health care program. In recognition of this remarkable woman's contribution to the diocese, St. Francis Xavier University granted her an honorary Doctor of Laws degree in 1950, and in the same year she was received in a private audience by Pope Pius XII.[76]

Frances MacIsaac of Brierly Brook stated that "the Sisters of St. Martha, through their hospitals, provided the people of eastern Nova Scotia with a form

Fig. 50 Mother Ignatius, first superior general of the Sisters of St. Martha, under who the Order's hospital services expanded and flourished. Courtesy Archives of the Sisters of St. Martha. 31.

164

of social health care long before the government got into the business." The charges for the medical services the sisters provided were low, and the sisters often insisted that the hospital board forgive the debts of needy people. This practice was particularly common during the Depression of the 1930s, when money was very scarce. Patients from rural communities who could not pay in cash for health care often paid in kind with vegetables and other farm products. Mothers with new babies were invited to remain in hospital for an extended stay at no extra cost in order to have a rest. In addition to the medical services provided by the doctors and nurses, there were sisters who spent their time consoling and caring for critically-ill patients and their relatives. They paid special attention to the spiritual needs of the sick. No patient was left to die alone. None of the relatives who took turns sitting with seriously ill family members went without lunch or tea.

The Sisters of St. Martha also made their mark in the area of social services in eastern Nova Scotia. In 1917, the Episcopal Corporation of the Diocese of Antigonish purchased property in Sydney and gave it to the sisters to enable them to start St. Mary's Home for orphans and neglected children.[77] This home was in response to the need created by the deaths of soldiers in World War I and by the deaths of so many during the Spanish flu epidemic of 1918. Demand for this facility was also created by parental desertion and the need to care for children of unmarried mothers.[78] Whole families of neglected, orphaned or homeless children were brought to the home. But the facility proved to be inadequate to meet the demands; in 1926, the Episcopal Corporation purchased a property in Bras d'Or where a new orphanage named the Little Flower Institute was opened for the care of "parentless and homeless little ones" over the age of two.[79] With this new facility, the sisters were able to devote St. Mary's Home exclusively to the care of infants.

Every effort was made to maintain a home-like atmosphere in these orphanages. One priest who visited the Little Flower orphanage stated: "Here there is spontaneity, laughter, freedom from restraint, and at the same time, there is the orderliness and good manners that come from training."[80] Each month a birthday party was held for children whose birthdays occurred during the month. Christmas was a festive occasion and the children gathered evergreens to make wreaths and garlands to decorate the orphan-

165

age. Before Christmas the orphans sent a letter to Santa published in *The Casket* to remind the people of eastern Nova Scotia not to forget them. An excerpt from one of these letters reads:

> There are about fifty of us, and we are the nicest bunch you ever saw. We like anything that little boys and girls ranging from one year to fifteen would, and we know that we will just love everything that you will bring. We are going to hang up our stockings, every one of us, even to the smallest, and that is why we are writing so you won't forget to call.[81]

On Christmas Eve, the older children stayed up for midnight mass. On Christmas morning, the toddlers awoke and came down for breakfast in housecoats and slippers to find many generous donations of gifts. Service organizations from the surrounding communities were particularly generous in their assistance.[82]

To help them develop a sense of responsibility and discipline, each child was assigned certain daily chores such as washing dishes, sweeping floors, carrying kindling and shoveling snow. Even with their efforts to provide the best of care, the sisters realized that an orphanage was no substitute for a good home, and so they made every effort to place these children with good families. Advertisements seeking homes for orphans frequently appeared in *The Casket.*

Fr. Jimmy Tompkins became concerned with the social problems of the people of Canso and persuaded the Sisters of St. Martha to open their first social welfare bureau in his parish in 1933.[83] Through this agency the sisters assisted the poor and the sick and encouraged self-help through adult education. From this initiation into organized social work, the sisters went on to work with the priests of the Diocese of Antigonish in developing and staffing social agencies in a number of parishes in Cape Breton. Many sisters who were practising social work were sent to take specialized courses at universities offering graduate programs in social work.

In 1935, the sisters responded to requests for social workers from the parishioners of Sacred Heart Parish and St. Theresa's Parish in Sydney and their services spread to all the parishes in industrial Cape Breton and some on the mainland.[84] The demands for social services were particularly pressing during the Depression.[85] The sisters provided grocery orders for the hungry, helped find jobs for the unemployed and sought accommodations for the homeless. Sister Mary MacDonald was a social worker in the industrial area during this period. She expressed amazement at the cooperation she received from the people of the community in her efforts to help. "Even though times were hard, I don't think I was ever refused assistance." The sisters also did a great deal of work with alcoholics. In cases where alcohol disrupted family life, the sisters went into the homes to see what they could do to help. Sr. Mary recalled that "Women and children often lived in fear of their men when they were drinking." The sisters intervened to try to comfort the women and children and to have a calming influence on the men.

The sisters provided service to unwed mothers by obtaining private homes for them to live in prior to their confinement. These homes were selected by a sister who was a trained social worker and the sisters provided a case worker to help the young women. In 1956, their focus on family welfare led to the development of a formal social service organization, the Family Service Bureau, that worked closely with social agencies in the communities it served in eastern Nova Scotia.

In 1958, the sisters opened a home for the aged in Antigonish named after R. K. MacDonald who made a major financial contribution to the building.[86] The commitment of the sisters to this venture was so strong that they mortgaged their motherhouse to finance the operation.

Fig. 51 Social workers in industrial Cape Breton. Courtesy Archives of the Sisters of St. Martha. 26.

Another contribution of the Sisters of St. Martha to the welfare of the people of eastern Nova Scotia was teaching. The sisters first entered school teaching at the request of Dr. Moses Coady of the Extension Department of St. Francis Xavier University. This move reflected his concern for the continuing depopulation of the rural areas of eastern Nova Scotia and the increasing tendency of the best qualified teachers to seek employment in urban areas or western Canada. Dr. Coady believed that improved teaching in rural schools would stop the decay of rural life.[87] He viewed the sisters to be suited to this task because they were "rural minded and had a special interest in improving social conditions."[88] Many of the sisters came from rural communities in eastern Nova Scotia and understood the problems of the people in these communities.

Although the Mother General of the Order was reluctant to take on responsibility for teaching at a time when the sisters were fully occupied with hospital and other charitable works, she eventually agreed to expand into that domain. St. FX offered incentive by providing free university education to those selected by the order to become teachers.[89] Many of the sisters who were interested in teaching took advantage of the opportunity to take courses and to pursue degrees and in so doing put well-educated teachers in the field. Selected sisters were sent to the University of Guelph, in Ontario, and to MacDonald College, in Quebec, to study home economics and rural development to prepare them to teach domestic science and agriculture. The professional qualifications of the teaching sisters were usually much higher than those of the lay teachers in rural schools.

Moved by the demand for their services, the sisters opened convents and staffed the public schools in Margaree Valley (1925), Bras d'Or (1926), St. Andrews (1927), Main-a-Dieu (1942), Heatherton (1951), South Ingonish and East Bay (1953), Dingwall (1955) and St. Peter's (1958).[90] In 1956, the congregation assigned teachers to the Post Road School and to the new St. Andrew Rural High School, both in Antigonish. Were it not for the services of the sisters, some of the small communities of eastern Nova Scotia and Cape Breton would not have had high school education available for their young people before the latter part of the 1950s.

These schools became an adjunct to the Extension Department of St. FX in organizing study clubs and in perpetuating the household arts of spinning, weaving, knitting and sewing. The sisters were also instrumental in initiating music and speech festivals so that their students could learn to perform in public.

The teaching assignments of the sisters in the rural schools were heavy, and the class sizes were large.[91] It was not uncommon for one sister to teach all academic subjects in grades ten, eleven and twelve. If they did not have sufficient academic background to teach certain subjects, they were expected to attend summer school to make up for these deficiencies. Because of the many grades and courses the sisters taught, they often offered extra classes to grade eleven and twelve students after school hours to prepare them for provincial examinations.

In some rural communities the congregation provided circuit teachers who spent a day a week in the rural schools of Antigonish and Guysboro teaching music, art and crafts.[92] Instruction in the fine arts carried over into extra-curricular activities and circuit teachers helped the regular classroom teachers prepare for Christmas concerts and musical performances. Other extra-curricular activities in rural schools were associated with 4-H organizations where students learned how to plant and care for gardens, look after farm animals and compete in public speaking.

In some of the more remote communities, living conditions for teachers were rustic and salaries extremely low. Sisters who taught in northern Cape Breton reported living in summer cottages before their convents were built. Most of these cottages had no insulation, running water or central heat. In winter the snow blocked the roads and isolated the communities from the outside world. Sr. Mary MacMullin, who taught in Dingwall in the early 1950s, laughed when she recalled how she carried a shovel to clear enough snow to make her way to school. In the northern communities where schools lacked central heat and janitorial services, the sisters and the pupils cleaned the classrooms and the outhouses, carried wood, started the fire, cleaned the ashes and kept the fire burning. The sisters accepted these conditions with good spirits and a sense of humour. According to Sr. MacMullin, "the cooperation of the students and the appreciation of their parents made it all worthwhile. There was a tremendous sense of community in the north."

Some teaching sisters recounted stories of how they provided help to poor and disadvantaged students.[93] These sisters tried to persuade the parents of these students to keep them in school, and they encouraged able students from among them to further their education. Poor children in rural communities could rarely obtain a university education, but the sisters gave financial aid or organized community activities to raise money to help them. Community benefactors always remained anonymous. The sisters at Bethany provided accommodations for needy students while they attended university, and in return for their room and board, these students did work at the motherhouse. Long after they graduated from university many of these students readily admitted

Fig. 52 Descending North Mountain, Cabot Trail, 1935. Courtesy Antigonish Heritage Museum. 2004.056.007.

that the encouragement and financial aid provided by the sisters made it possible for them to obtain an education.

At first, St. Martha's congregation looked upon its teaching sisters as a burden on over-stretched finances. After all, teaching did not command sufficient income to enable the sisters to provide for their own keep, and financing the teaching sisters was diverting funds from the order's first priority, which was hospital work. But in the 1950s, a marked improvement in teachers' salaries enabled the teaching sisters to make significant financial contributions to the upkeep of their expensive hospitals.

The work of the sisters in adult education was an extension of their teaching mission. Dr. Coady encouraged the Sisters of St. Martha to become involved in the work of the Extension Department of St. Francis Xavier University. In 1932, he opened a women's section of the Department and placed Sr. Marie Michael MacKinnon in charge of it.[94] Her chief work involved directing study clubs for women, supplying information, editing the women's section of the Extension Bulletin and promoting handicrafts.

The services of the Sisters of St. Martha were concentrated in eastern Nova Scotia and contributed greatly to improving the lives of the people there. Through their hospitals they brought health care and nursing education; through their social services they looked after the poor and the disadvantaged; and through their teaching services to small rural communities they brought young people a high-school education that would not otherwise have been available to them.

Notes

Notes on Chapter 1
1. Ross, *The Folklore of the Scottish Highlands*, 12.
2. Skene, *The Highlanders of Scotland*, 45.
3. Dunn, *Highland Settler*, 3.
4. Campbell and MacLean, *Beyond the Atlantic Roar*, 13.
5. Hunter, *The Making of the Crofting Community*, 7-9.
6. Grant, *Highland Folkways*, 198-211.
7. Campbell, *Canna*, 48.
8. MacKinnon, *The Scottish Highlanders*, 97-98.
9. Campbell, *Gaelic in Scottish Education and Life*, 40.
10. Campbell, *Canna*, 88.
11. Anson, *Underground Catholicism in Scotland*, 101.
12. Campbell, *Canna*, 88.
13. From the 1764-1765 Census of the Small Islands, Archives, University of Edinburgh.
14. Prebble, *Culloden*, 128-129.
15. Ibid., 205.
16. MacKay, *Scotland Farewell*, 9.
17. Ibid., 9.
18. D.L. MacDonald, "The Influence of the Scottish Culture," *The Casket* , 17 July 1941, 5.
19. MacLean, *Highlanders*, 225.
20. MacKay, 11.
21. Hunter, 9.
22. Donaldson, *The Scots Overseas*, 58.
23. Sinclair, "Highland Emigration to Nova Scotia," *The Casket*, 9 September 1943, 9.
24. Bumstead, *The People's Clearance*, 34-35.
25. MacLean, 225.
26. A. H. Smith, "Through the Dark Night: The Story of the Survival of Catholicism in the Highlands and Islands of Scotland," *The Casket*, 24 February 1938, 10.
27. Anson, 146.
28. Ibid., 168.
29. Lockhead, *The Scots' Household in the Eighteenth Century*, 152.
30. Anson, 159.
31. Ibid., 340.
32. Bumstead, 95.
33. Sinclair, 9.
34. Ibid, 8.
35. Anson, 172.
36. Bumstead, 218.
37. Transactions of the Celtic Congress, comp. Phillips, 10.
38. "The Sutherland Clearances," *The Casket*, 17 March 1938, 2.

39. Ibid., 2.
40. MacKenzie, *The History of the Highland Clearances,* 25.
41. Ibid., 20.
42. Campbell, *The Book of Barra,* 74.
43. MacKenzie, 220.
44. Anson, 245.
45. MacKenzie, 263-64.
46. Bumstead, 95.
47. Sinclair, 8.
48. MacArthur, "Some Emigrant Ships from the Western Highlands," *Transactions of the Gaelic Society of Inverness,* LV, 325.
49. Bumstead, 217.
50. Martell, *Immigration to and Emigration from Nova Scotia, 1815-1838.*
51. Dunn, 17-18
52. MacLeod, "Why Did the Highland Scots Emigrate to Nova Scotia?" *The Cape Breton Post,* 22 July 1960, 6.
53. An example of the practice of telling stories about the crossing is cited in "Pioneer Days in Pictou," *The Casket,* 13 January 1928, 4.

Notes on Chapter 2
1. This news account was reprinted in *The Celtic Magazine,* ix, No. xcviii, 23.
2. "Hebrides and Canada," *The Casket,* 2 May 1924, 10.
3. MacDonald, *History of Antigonish County,* 1876, 15.
4. Martell, 19.
5. Archibald, "Early Scottish Settlers in Cape Breton," *Collections of the Nova Scotia Historical Society,* 1914, 79.
6. MacKay, 87.
7. MacDonald, 15.
8. From the Gaelic newspaper *Mac-Talla,* 3, No. 1, 6.
9. Archibald, 79.
10. Bumstead, 143-47.
11. MacKay, 221.
12. Ibid., xii.
13. Patterson, *A History of the County of Pictou,* 55-57.
14. Archibald, 79-80.
15. Patterson, 57.
16. Ibid., 144.
17. "Pioneer Days in Pictou," *The Casket,* 12 January 1928, 4.
18. MacKay, 139.
19. Gilbert, "The Scottish Servant in Early America," *The Highlander,* 10.
20. Ibid., 4.
21. MacDonald, "Early Highland Emigration to Nova Scotia and Prince Edward Island from 1770-1853," Nova Scotia Historical Society, V. 23, 1909, p. 47.
22. Campbell and MacLean, 61.
23. *The Casket,* 10 March 1938, 10.

24. C. I. N. MacLeod, "Why Did the Highland Scots Emigrate to Nova Scotia?" *Cape Breton Post*, 22 July 1960, 6.
25. Campbell and MacLean, 21.
26. C. S. MacDonald, 115.
27. *The Casket*, 16 September 1943, 8.
28. Martell, 9.
29. *The Casket*, 5 July 1928, 11.
30. Fergusson, ed., Uniake's Sketches of Cape Breton and Other Papers Relating to Cape Breton Island, 1862-65, 179.
31. Martell, 50.
32. Ibid., 9.
33. Stanley, *The Well-Watered Garden*, 20.
34. MacNeil, "Scottish Settlement in Colonial Nova Scotia: A Case Study of Saint. Andrew's Township," *Scottish Tradition*, 64.
35. Martell, 7.
36. Ibid., 14.
37. Patterson, 89.
38. McLaren, 52.
39. Patterson, 89.
40. This description of these homes was obtained through interviews with descendants of the pioneers.
41. *The Casket*, 11 February 1858, 6.
42. MacDougall, *History of Inverness County*, 4-5.
43. The Casket, 13 January 1949, 6.
44. MacDonald, *Sketches of Highlanders*, viii.
45. MacKay, 154.
46. *The Casket*, 26 November 1931, 4.

Notes on Chapter 3
1. Skene, 118.
2. MacLeod, 10.
3. Skene, 118.
4. Coghill, *The Elusive Gael*, 26-27.
5. Fraser, *Folklore of Nova Scotia*, xii.
6. D. MacGillivray, "Development of Highland Education," in *Leabhar A'Chlachain, Home Life of the Highlanders, 1400-1746*, 81.
7. Fraser, xiii.
8. Stewart, *Sketches of the Character, Manners, and Present State of the Highlanders of Scotland*, 98-99.
9. MacLellan, 51.
10. MacLeod, 15.
11. Ross, 84.
12. MacLeod, 36.
13. Ross, 39.
14. Dunn, 46.

15. *The Casket*, 26 November 1931, 4.
16. *The Casket*, 17 March 1938, 2.
17. Calum MacLeod addresses this tradition and records some of the folk tales he collected in *Highland Scottish Folklore and Beliefs and in Stories from Nova Scotia*.
18. Coghill, 26.
19. Skene, 133.
20. Ibid., 134.
21. MacLean, *The Literature of the Highlands*, 9.
22. Ibid., 10.
23. MacLeod, 27.
24. Ibid., 77.
25. MacDonald, "Music in the Home Life of the Gael," *Transactions of the Gaelic Society of Inverness*, 278.
26. Munroe, "The Music of the Clans," in *Leabhar A'Chlachain, Home Life of the Highlanders, 1400-1746*, 115.
27. Ibid., 121.
28. Whyte, "The Songs of the Gael," in *The Old Highlands*, 329.
29. MacLeod, "Hebridean Folk Songs," *Scottish Studies*, 63.
30. Creighton and MacLeod, *Gaelic Songs of Nova Scotia*, 32.
31. MacDonnell, *The Emigrant Experience*, 15.
32. MacDonald, "Music in the Home Life of the Gael," *Transactions of the Gaelic Society of Inverness*, 279.
33. M. MacLean, 233.
34. Ross, 14.
35. MacKenzie, 46.
36. Ibid., 46- 47.
37. *The Casket*, 10 January 1943,
38. Dunn, 48.
39. *The Casket*, 7 December 1939, 10.
40. MacLellan, 47.
41. Ross, 15-16.
42. Description of the celebration of Christmas in eastern Nova Scotia obtained through interviews with Highland Scottish women.
43. Ross, 119.
44. Ibid., 116.
45. Polson, *Our Highland Folklore Heritage*, 145.
46. MacKenzie-Campbell, *Highland Village on the Bras d'or*, 42-3.
47. "Late Nineteenth and Early Twientieth Century Weddings," n.p.
48. Ross, 107-108.
49. MacLeod, 33.
50. Patterson, 244
51. Whidden, 160.
52. Jephcott et al., *The Postal History of Nova Scotia and New Brunswick*, 61.
53. *The Casket*, 2 June 1927, 6.
54. Cameron, *Pictou County's History*, 67.
55. Whidden, 116.

56. Cameron, *Pictou County's History*, 68.
57. M. MacDonnell, "The Contribution of the Congregation de Notre Dame to the Scottish Gaelic 'Renaissance' in Nova Scotia," 3.
58. Cameron, *Pictou County's History*, 68.
59. Whidden, *The History of the Town of Antigonish*, 160.
60. "The History of the Telephone in Nova Scotia," n.p.
61. Cameron, *Pictou County's History*, 52-53.
62. Johnston, 85.
63. *The Casket*, 9 December 1880, 2.
64. Cameron, *Pictou County's History*, 53-54.
65. Dunn, 136-149.
66. Turner, "Canadian Mosaic," 30-31
67. J. D. Cameron, 322.

Notes on Chapter 4
1. Urquhart and Ellington, Eigg, 20.
2. Donaldson, *The Scottish Reformation*, 77-84.
3. Moir, *Enduring Witness: A History of the Presbyterian Church in Canada*, 171-179.
4. Reid, "The Scottish Presbyterian Tradition," in *The Scottish Tradition in Canada*, 120.
5. Cameron, *Pictou County's History*, 21.
6. Ibid., 21.
7. Moir, 214.
8. MacKinnon, *The History of the Presbyterian Church in Cape Breton*, 9.
9. Moir, 27.
10. Information from records in the Public Archives of Nova Scotia reprinted in Stanley, *The Well-Watered Garden*, 30.
11. Ibid., 2.
12. Stanley, 34.
13. Ibid., 43.
14. Ibid., 64-85.
15. Murray, "Relief and Charity to Immigrants in Cape Breton, 1820-1880," 5.
16. Stanley, 133.
17. Ibid., 134.
18. Donaldson, 149.
19. Stanley, 141-45.
20. Dunn, 99.
21. Moir, 179.
22. Mitchinson, "Canadian Women and Church Missionary Societies in the Nineteenth Century," *Atlantis*, 58-59.
23. Ibid., 58.
24. *Cape Breton Post*, 9 September 2006, C3.
25. Moir, 179.
26. MacKinnon, 164-168.
27. *Cape Breton Post*, 9 September 2006, C3.
28. Moir, 164.

29. Patterson, 158-59.
30. Cameron, *More About New Glasgow*, 127.
31. Ibid, 287.
32. Dunn, 99.
33. Statistics from the Public Archives of Nova Scotia reproduced in Stanley, 29-30.
34. Ibid.
35. Johnston, Vol 1, 142.
36. Ibid., 139-140.
37. Ibid., 158.
38. *The Casket*, 22 July 1943, p. 9.
39. Stanley, 32.
40. Johnston, 346.
41. Plessis, *The Plessis Diary of 1811 and 1812*," 78.
42. Excerpt from "*The Plessis Diary of 1811 and 1812*," reproduced in Johnston, vol. 1, 231.
43. Johnston, Vol. 1, 81.
44. Martin, 105.
45. Johnston, *A History of the Catholic Church in Eastern Nova Scotia*, Vol. II, 198.
46. Ibid., 205-15.
47. Ibid., 330-31.
48. Ibid., 416.
49. MacLean, Bishop John Cameron: *Piety and Politics*, 146.
50. Information about the involvement of women in the social activities of the Catholic church was obtained through interviews.
51. Grant, *Highland Folk Ways*, 129.

Notes on Chapter 5
1. Information on the attitude toward wedlock in the Highlands was obtained from MacKenzie, "The Social Life of the Community," in *Leabhar A'Chlachain, Home Life of the Highlanders, 1400-1746*, 49.
2. Carr, *Tour Through Scotland in 1807*, 439.
3. Johnston, *A History of the Catholic Church in Eastern Nova Scotia*, vol. 2, 289.
4. Henderson, "The Women of the Glen: Some Thoughts on Highland History," in *The Celtic Consciousness*, 256.
5. MacNeil, "Scottish Settlement in Colonial Nova Scotia," *Scottish Tradition*, 65.
6. Information obtained through interviews with the relatives of single women.
7. Stewart, *Sketches of the Character, Manners, and Present State of the Highlanders of Scotland*, 91.
8. Information about families was obtained through interviews.
9. Information obtained from obituaries in *The Casket*.
10. Detailed information about the domestic activities of Highland women was obtained through interviews.
11. *The Casket*, 14 August 1853, 2.

12. Cameron, *Pictou County's History*, 105.
13. Information about the handling of food was obtained through interviews with Highland women.
14. MacLeod, *Stories from Nova Scotia*, 50.
15. MacDonald, *Sketches of Highlanders: With an Account of Their Early Arrival in North America*, viii.
16. Nova Scotia, Legislative Assembly, *Journal of Proceedings of the House of Assembly of the Province of Nova Scotia*, Appendix No. 8, "Agriculture," 31.
17. Nova Scotia Department of Agriculture, "Antigonish County, Nova Scotia: A Study of Land Utilization, Farm Production, and Rural Living," Bulletin No. 118, 47.
18. *The Casket*, 19 October 1905, 2.
19. *The Casket*, 30 August 1900, 6.
20. Sister Mairi MacDonald wrote this description of Highland food in her Introduction to Recollections, n.p.
21. Ibid., n.p.
22. *The Casket*, 24 July 1890, 1.
23. *The Casket*, 1 May 1902, 2.
24. Information about folk remedies was obtained through interviews with Highland women.
25. Information about the preparation of clothing was obtained through interviews with Highland women.
26. MacNeil, *The Highland Heart in Nova Scotia*, 57.
27. Campbell, *Highland Village on the Bras d'or*, 38.
28. *The Casket*, 28 February 1946, 9.
29. *The Casket*, 1 July 1871, 4.
30. Nova Scotia Department of Agriculture, 61.
31. Ibid., 61.
32. J. M. Cameron, 235.
33. Dunn, 57.
34. Cameron, *More About New Glasgow*, 28.
35. From "The Engineers Report on the Antigonish Water Works," *The Casket*, 10 September 1891, 1.
36. Province of Nova Scotia, "Royal Commission: Provincial Economic Inquiry," 85.
37. Cameron, *Pictou County's History*, 244.
38. Whidden, "The History of the Town of Antigonish," 163.
39. Ryan, "Electrification of Nova Scotia Homes," 23.
40. Ibid., 46.
41. Ibid., 64-69.
42. Brady, "Electric Power," in Report of the Royal Commission on Provincial Development and Rehabilitation, 24-5.
43. Province of Nova Scotia, 76.
44. Ryan, 72.

Notes on Chapter 6
1. Pennant, *A Tour in Scotland*, 49.

2. *The Casket*, 9 September 1943, 13

3. MacLellan, 29.

4. Anecdotes that illustrate the welfare role of the family were obtained through interviews with elderly Highland women.

5. Information about how the homeless and the elderly were looked after was obtained through inteviews.

6. Information obtained from interviews with lawyers.

7. Nova Scotia Department of Public Welfare, S. Fitzner, "The Development of Social Welfare in Nova Scotia," 51.

8. Testimony to ability of a widow with a young family to survive is to be found in M. MacLellan's family history, The Glen, 32-35.

9. Muise, "The Industrial Context of Inequality: Female Participation in Nova Scotia's Paid Labor Force, 1871-1971," *Acadiensis*, 16.

10. *The Casket*, 7 January 1937, 7.

11. Guest, The Emergence of Social Security in Canada, 9.

12. Nova Scotia Legislature, *Revised Statutes of Nova Scotia*, Vol. 1, 430-434.

13. MacKenzie, "Antigonish Poor Farm and Asylum--Antigonish," in *Poverty, Poor Houses, and Philanthropy*, 75.

14. Morton, "Older Women and Their Place in Nova Scotia, 1881-1931," *Atlantis*, 26.

15. Morton, 27.

16. Ibid., 29.

17. MacKenzie, 74.

18. Nova Scotia, Legislative Assembly, J*ournal of Proceedings of the House of Assembly of the Province of Nova Scotia*, Session 1889, 11.

19. Ibid., Appendix B, "Public Charities," 7-8.

20. Nova Scotia, Legislative Assembly, J*ournal and Proceedings of the House of Assembly of the Province of Nova Scotia*, Session 1922, Appendix No. 3 D, 40.

21. MacKenzie, 76.

22. *The Casket*, 6 January 1949, 10.

23. House of Commons Special Committee on Social Security, "Report on Social Security for Canada," 69.

24. Ibid., 69.

25. Fitzner, 51.

26. Guest, 130-31.

27. *The Casket*, 6 January 1949, 10.

28. Nova Scotia Legislative Assembly, *Journal of Proceedings of the House of Assembly of the Province of Nova Scotia*, Part II , 1929, 123.

29. Cameron, *More about New Glasgow*, 244-55.

30. Ibid., 255.

31. Pierson, "Women and the War Effort," 111.

32. Geller, "The Wartime Elections Act of 1917 and the Canadian Women's Movement," *Atlantis*, 103.

33. *The Halifax Herald*, 5 December 1918, 4.

34. *The Casket*, 13 May 1943, 6.

35. *The Casket*, 17 July 1941. 5.

36. Pierson. "Women and the War Effort," 111.
37. *The Casket*, 13 May 1943, 2.
38. Bland, "Henrietta the Homemaker and 'Rosie the Riveter,': Images of Women in Advertising in MacLean's Magazine, 1939 to 1950," *Atlantis*, 67.

Notes on Chapter 7
1. Wylie, "Coal Culture," 11.
2. Cameron, 134.
3. Frank, "The Cape Breton Coal Miners, 1917- 1926," (PhD diss.), 74.
4. Royal Commission on Canada's Economic Prospects, The Nova Scotia Coal Industry, 19-20.
5. Ryan, Women's Unpaid Work: A Case Study of Coal Miners' Wives and Widows, 77-80.
6. "Report of the Royal Commission on Coal, 1946," 299.
7. Wylie, 137.
8. Ibid., 171.
9. Ryan, 24.
10. "Report of the Royal Commission Respecting the Coal Mines of the Province of Nova Scotia, 1925," 41-42.
11. Ryan, 30.
12. "Report of the Royal Commission Respecting the Coal Mines of the Province of Nova Scotia, 1925," 41.
13. Ibid., 41.
14. Ibid.
15. Wylie, 172.
16. Information regarding the life of miners and their wives on small farms was obtained through interviews with their children.
17. "Report of the Royal Commission Respecting the Coal Mines of the Province of Nova Scotia, 1925," 45.
18. Ibid., 46.
19. Ryan, 69.
20. Ibid., 48.
21. Ibid., 129.
22. This information was obtained through interviews with children of miners.
23. "Report of the Royal Commission on Coal, 1946," 298.
24. Ryan, 59.
25. Wylie, 98.
26. Twohig, An Analysis of Workers in Nova Scotia, 1881-1921, 98.
27. Alexander, "A Preliminary Review of the History of Coal Mining in Nova Scotia," 21.
28. Wylie, 98.
29. Ibid., 98-99.
30. Information about the aspirations of the miners and their wives for their children was obtained through interviews with their children.
31. Ryan, 21.

32. Wylie, "Coal Culture," 134.
33. Frank, 86.
34. Dunn, 132.
35. J. M. Cameron, *Pictou County's History*, 140.
36. Forsey, "Economic and Social Aspects of the Nova Scotia Coal Industry," 9.
37. "Report of the Royal Commission on Coal, 1946," 296.
38. Information from the D. S. Morrison papers, Beaton Institute.
39. Ryan, 117.
40. Wylie, 109.
41. Frank, 101.
42. Boyle, *Father Tompkins of Nova Scotia*, 89.
43. *The Casket*, 19 May 1921, 3.
44. Wylie, 112.
45. Ryan, 92-93.
46. *The Casket*, 19 March 1925, 8.
47. MacSween, "Coal Mining in Cape Breton," 8.
48. Ibid., 2.
49. Earle, "A Preliminary Review of Nova Scotia's Historical Economic Context," 38.
50. Wylie, 172.
51. Ryan, 34.
52. Boyle, 198.
53. Ryan, 86.
54. Wylie, 13.
55. J. M. Cameron, *Pictou County's History*, 111.
56. C. S. Cameron, *The Iron and Steel Industry in Canada*, 221.
57. Ibid., 222.
58. C. S. Cameron, 225.
59. The Board of Temperance and Moral Reform of the Methodist Church and the Board of Social Services and Evangelism of the Presbyterian Church, Sydney, Nova Scotia: The Report of a Brief Investigation of Social Conditions in the City, 4.
60. Twohig, 79.
61. Crawley, "Class Conflict and the Establishment of the Sydney Steel Industry, 1899-1904" in T*he Island: New Perspectives on Cape Breton History, 1713-1990*, 152.
62. Twohig, 88.
63. D. MacGillivray, "Industrial Unrest in Cape Breton, 1919-1925," (MA thesis), 93.
64. The Board of Temperance and Moral Reform of the Methodist Church and the Board of Social Services and Evangelism of the Presbyterian Church, 14.
65. Ibid., 86.
66. Ibid.
67. Report of the Commission Appointed under Order in Council, 1923, The Industrial Unrest among the Steel Workers at Sydney, Nova Scotia, 22.
68. Cameron, *Pictou County's History*, 112.

69. Crawley, 154.
70. Crawley, 157.
71. Earle, *A preliminary Review of Nova Scotia's Historical Economic Context*, 35-36.
72. Earle, A Preliminary Report on Unionization and Strikes in Nova Scotia, 1880-1980, 78.
73. "Report of the Commission Appointed under Order in Council," 1923, 8.
74. "Report of the Commission Appointed Under Order in Council," 1923, 15.
75. Earle, A Preliminary Report on Unionization and Strikes in Nova Scotia, 1880-1980, 78.
76. MacGillivray, 112.
77. Heron, Working in Steel, 157.
78. Earle, A Preliminary Report on Unionization and Strikes in Nova Scotia, 1880-1980, 79.
79. Earle, "A Preliminary Review of Nova Scotia's Historical Economic Context, 1920-1980," 47.
80. A list of the names of the women who worked in the steel plant is avail able from the Beaton Institute.
81. Information on the female steel workers was obtained from taped interviews at the Beaton Institute.
82. From an interview with Catherine Chisholm who held a managerial position during World War Two.
83. Information about the domestic and social lives of the wives of the steel workers was obtained through interviews.

Notes on Chapter 8
1. Muise, 13-14.
2. Ibid., 14.
3. Ryan, History of Women in Office Work in Nova Scotia. n.p.
4. Ibid.
5. Ibid.
6. Campbell and MacLean, 109.
7. Dunn, 126.
8. Campbell and MacLean, 109.
9. Adams, "Highland Emigrations of 1783--1903," *The Scottish Historical Review*, 123.
10. *The Casket*, 27 March 1919, 2.
11. Thorton, "The Problem of Out-migration from Atlantic Canada, 1871-1921," *Acadiensis*, 18. 19.
12. Beattie, "Going Up to Lynn," *Acadiensis*, 85.
13. Nilsen, *The Nova Scotia Gael in Boston*, 83.
14. Dunn, 126.
15. *The Casket*, 27 March 1890, 3.
16. Beattie, 67-68.
17. Ibid., 69.
18. Interviews with former domestics and their relatives and friends.

19. Beattie, 69.
20. Iinterviews with relatives and friends of domestics.
21. Pierson, "Ladies or Loose Women," *Atlantis*, 246.
22. From interviews with educated women.
23. Ibid.
24. Martin, ed., *The Catholic Diocesan Directory of Nova Scotia*, 129.
25. *The Casket*, April 1, 1886, 1.
26. P. Butts, "Pilgrimage from France to Montreal to Antigonish," A supplement to *The Casket*, 26 April 1955, 50-54.
27. "The Antigonish Province of the Sisters of Charity," Antigonish Province Convent Histories, Archives, Motherhouse of the Sisters of Charity.
28. "Mount Saint Bernard Centennial, 1883-1983," 21.
29. C. B. Fergusson, "The Inaguration of the Free School System in Nova Scotia," 1964, 6-25.
30. Guilford, "Separate Spheres," *Acadiensis*, 44.
31. Muise, 26.
32. Guilford, 49.
33. MacKay, *Annual Report of the Superintendent of Education of Nova Scotia*, xxvii.
34. Butts, 48-49.
35. J. D. Cameron, 96.
36. Rankin, *A History of the County of Antigonish, Nova Scotia*, 69.
37. MacKay, xxvii.
38. J. Guilford, "Family Strategies and Professional Careers: The Experience of Women Teachers in Nineteenth Century Nova Scotia," Dawson Lecture Series, 15-16.
39. An example of such ads is to be found in *The Casket*, 4 August 1910, 8.
40. Muise, 27.
41. Guilford, 16-17.
42. Muise, 28.
43. Guilford, 11.
44. Report of the Royal Commission on Education, Public Service and Provincial-Municipal Relations, 1974, Summary and Recommendations, 6.
45. Guilford, 13.
46. Fergusson, "Inaguration of the Free School System in Nova Scotia," *Journal of Education*, 23.
47. Report of the Royal Commission on Education, Public Service and Provincial-Municipal Relations, 1974, 16.
48. Moffatt, "One Hundred Years of Free Schools," *Journal of Education*, 30.
49. Guilford, 63.
50. Muise, 27.
51. Information about living conditions and social life were obtained through interviews with former teachers.
52. Moffatt, 32.
53. Ibid., 33.
54. Ibid., 33-34.

55. Ibid., 33.
56. Ibid.
57. V. J. Pottier. Commissioner, "Report of the Royal Commission on Public School Finances in Nova Scotia," 18-32.
58. Ibid., 39-40.
59. J. D. Cameron, 252.
60. J. M. Cameron, *More About New Glasgow*, 275.
61. Keddy et al., "The Nurse as Mother Surrogate," *Health Care for Women International*, 181.
62. Robson, 47.
63. Royal Commission on Health Services, Mussallem, Nursing Education in Canada, 6.
64. Ibid., 10.
65. Dolan, *History of Nursing*, 340.
66. Dryden, *Nursing Trends*, 4.
67. RNANS Entry to Practice Committee, "Historical Perspective on Nursing Education," 1.
68. Mussallem, 7.
69. Lyons, "History of Nursing Education in Nova Scotia," 1.
70. Ibid., 4.
71. Ibid.
72. J. M. Cameron, "Major Margaret C. MacDonald, R. R. C.," An obituary in *The Eastern Chronicle*, 15 September 1948, 2.
73. Ibid.

Notes on Chapter 9
1. Martin, 133.
2. O'Grady, "A Century of Education," 7.
3. "Congregation de Notre Dame in the Maritimes," 3.
4. Ibid.
5. "History of Stella Maris Convent," 2.
6. Butts, 54.
7. Ibid.
8. Martin, 129.
9. *The Casket*, 28 July 1927, 18.
10. Johnston, Vol. II, 334.
11. "Report of the Superintendent of Education," *Journal of Education*, 1884, 29.
12. J. D. Cameron, 78.
13. *The Casket*, 1 April 1886. 1.
14. An example of the prize offerings for Mount St. Bernard is to be found in *The Casket*, 26 June 1947, 12.
15. Martin, 129.
16. "Mount St. Bernard Centennial, 1883-1983," p. 21.
17. This statement from *The Casket* was reprinted in J. D. Cameron, *For the People: A History of St. Francis Xavier University*, 97.
18. "Mount St. Bernard Centennial, 1883-1983," 22.

19. Ibid., 23.
20. This information was obtained from Highland Scottish women or their daughters who attended Mount St. Bernard.
21. "St. Peter's Convent, Port Hood: Arrival of the First Sisters," n.p.
22. Ibid., 2.
23. *The Casket*, 27 October 1887, 2.
24. "St. Joseph's Convent, Mabou: One Hundred Years of Christian Education," 6-12.
25. *Inverness News*, 23 June 1905, n.p.
26. Butts, 49-54.
27. "Annals," Holy Angels Convent, 1885-1921, n.p.
28. Ibid.
29. MacDonnell, "The Contribution of the Congregation de Notre Dame to the Scottish Gaelic 'Rennaissance' in Nova Scotia," 6-7.
30. Ibid., 7.
31. "Sisters of Charity: Antigonish Diocese,1849-1949," 5.
32. Ibid., 7.
33. Ibid.
34. "Annals," Our Lady of Lourdes Convent, 3.
35. "Sisters of Charity" Antigonish Diocese, 1849-1949," 7.
36. Kirincich, "Our Lady of Lourdes Church, 1883-1983," 36-38.
37. Ibid., 76.
38. Ibid., 29-32.
39. "Remembering into the Future," 2-4.
40. Ibid., 8-9.
41. "Annals, Hamilton Memorial Hospital, 1937-1938," 13.
42. "Remembering into the Future," 13.
43. "Sisters of Charity: Antigonish Diocese, 1849-1949," 8.
44. "St. Anne's Parish, 1866- 1966," n.p.
45. "Sisters of Charity: Antigonish Diocese, 1849-1949," 9.
46. McKenna, "The Sisters of Charity, Halifax: Their Legacy of Service to the Diocese of Antigonish, 1882-1994," 6.
47. *The Mail Star*, 9 May 1964, 8.
48. *Folia Montana*, July, 1986, 8.
49. Ibid.
50. Boyle, 217.
51. McKenna, 7.
52. Ibid., 5.
53. Ibid., 15.
54. Ibid.
55. Letter from Bishop Cameron to the Diocesan Clergy, 1894.
56. Fultz, "The Marthas: A Story of Pioneering Faith," 3-5.
57. Information obtained from lists of the names of postulants in the Bethany Archives.
58. Information obtained from responses of the pioneer sisters to a questionnaire from Mother Ignatius in 1946.

59. Information obtained through interviews with graduates of St. Francis Xavier University.
60. *The Xavieran Annual*, 7.
61. P. F. Martin, 122-123.
62. "Nursing Education," n.p.
63. "Nursing Education: The Two-Year Collegiate Program," 3
64. Articles of Agreement, between the Sisters of St. Martha and the Governors of St. Francis Xavier University, 1917.
65. Martin, 122.
66. Kelly, "Farewell to St. Joseph's Hospital," n.p.
67. "St. Joseph's Hospital," 1-2.
68. Kelly, 2.
69. "Data—St. Rita's Hospital," 1.
70. "St. Mary's Hospital, 1925-1977," n.p.
71. Interview with retired nursing sisters.
72. MacMahon, "St. Martha's School of Nursing," n.p.
73. "Biographical sketch of Mother Ignatius," n.p.
74. The accomplishments of Mother Ignatius were outlined in Dr. Somer's homily delivered at a mass celebrating the golden jubilee of her profession. September, 1962.
75. Ibid.
76. Ibid.
77. Martin, 125.
78. "St. Mary's Infant Home, Sydney" *Little Flower Messenger*, 4.
79. Martin, 125.
80. St. Mary's Infany Hone, Sydney," 4.
81. The Casket, 20 December 1934, 8.
82. "Little Flower Institute: Historical Highlights," 5-6.
83. Martin, 126.
84. "Family Service Bureau: St. Theresa's Parish, Sydney," n.p.
85. "Bethany Annals," n.p.
86. Martin, 125.
87. "Notes on the Founding and Growth of the Margaree Forks School," n.p.
88. Letter from Dr. Coady to the General Superior, Rev. Mother Stanislaus, August 4, 1923.
89. Information on the teaching credentials of the teaching sisters was obtained through interviews with retired teaching sisters.
90. Martin, 125.
91. Information about the work load of the teaching sisters was obtained through interviews with retired teaching sisters.
92. Information about the efforts of the teachers to promote the arts was obtained through conversations with retired teachers.
93. Information about measures to help poor and disadvantaged students was obtained through conversations with retired teaching sisters.
94. "A General View of the Religious Life," 16.

Bibliography

Books

Anson, Peter F. *Underground Catholicism in Scotland.* Montrose: Standard Press, 1970.

Boyle, George. *Father Tompkins of Nova Scotia.* New York: P. J. Kenedy and Sons, 1953.

Bumstead, J. M. *The People's Clearance: Highland Emigration to British North America.* Edinburgh: Edinburgh University Press, 1982.

Cameron, James D. *For the People: A History of St. Francis Xavier University.* Montreal:and Kingston: Mc Gill-Queen's University Press, 1998.

Cameron, James M. *More About New Glasgow.* Kentville: Kentville Publishing Co., 1972.

———. *Pictou County's History.* Kentville: Kentville Publishing Co., 1972.

Campbell, Douglas and Ray MacLean. *Beyond the Atlantic Roar: A Study of the Nova Scotia Scots.* Toronto: McClelland and Stewart, 1974.

Campbell, John Lorne. *Canna: The Story of a Hebridean Island.* Oxford: Oxford University Press, 1984.

———. *Gaelic in Scottish Education and Life.* Edinburgh: W. and A. K. Johnston, 1945.

———, ed. *The Book of Barra.* London: Routledge and Sons, 1936.

Carr, John. *Tour Through Scotland in 1807.* London: W. Clowes, 1809.

Coghill, Dugald. *The Elusive Gael.* Stirling: Eneas MacKay, 1928.

Crawley, Ron. "Class Conflict and the Establishment of the Sydney Steel Industry, 1899-1904" in *The Island: New Perspectives on Cape Breton History, 1713-1990,* edited by Kenneth Donovan, 148-63. Sydney: Nova Scotia: Acadiensis Press, 1990.

Creighton, Helen and Calum MacLeod. *Gaelic Songs of Nova Scotia.* Ottawa: Queen's Printer, 1964.

Dolan, Josephine A. *History of Nursing.* 12th ed. Philadelphia: W. B. Saunders, 1969.

Donaldson, Gordon. *The Scots Overseas.* London: Robert Hale, 1966.

———. *The Scottish Reformation.* Cambridge: Cambridge University Press, 1979.

Dunn, Charles W. *Highland Settler: A Portrait of the Scottish Gael in Cape Breton and Eastern Nova Scotia.* Toronto: University of Toronto Press, 1953.

Fraser, Mary L. *Folklore of Nova Scotia.* Antigonish: Formac, 1975.

Grant, Isabel F. *Highland Folkways*. London: Routledge and Kegan Paul, 1961.

Guest, Dennis. *The Emergence of Social Security in Canada*. Vancouver: University of British Columbia Press, 1980.

Henderson, Hannish. "The Women of the Glen: Some Thoughts on Highland History," in *The Celtic Consciousness*, edited by Robert O'Driscoll, 255-81. Toronto: MacLelland and Stewart, 1978.

Henderson, Virginia. "The Nature of Nursing," in *Nursing Trends*, edited by M. Virginia Dryden., 14-18. Iowa: Wm. C. Brown, 1968.

Heron, Craig. *Working in Steel: The Early years in Canada, 1883-1935*. Toronto: MacLelland and Stewart, 1988.

Hunter, James. *The Making of the Crofting Community*. Edinburgh: John Donald, 1976.

Jephcott, C.M., V. G. Greene and J. H. M. Young. *The Postal History of Nova Scotia and New Brunswick*. Toronto: Sessons, 1964.

Johnston, Angus A. *A History of the Catholic Church in Eastern Nova Scotia*. vol. 1. Antigonish: St. Francis Xavier University Press, 1960.

————. *A history of the Catholic Church in Eastern Nova Scotia, 1827-1880*. vol. 2. Antigonish: St. Francis Xavier University Press, 1971.

Lockhead, Marion. *The Scots' Household in the Eighteenth Century*. Edinburgh: The Moray Press, 1948.

MacDonald, Mairi. Introduction to *Recollections*, edited by R. A. MacLean, Antigonish: Casket Printing and Publishing Co., 1978.

MacDonald, J.W. *History of Antigonish County, 1876*. Anigonish: Formac, 1975.

MacDonald, R.C. *Sketches of Highlanders: With an Account of Their Early Arrival in North America*. St. John, New Brunswick: Henry Chubb and Company, 1843.

MacDonnell, Margaret. *The Emigrant Experience: Songs of Highland Emigrants in North America*. Toronto: University of Toronto Press, 1982.

MacDougall, John L. *History of Inverness County*. Belleville, Ontario: Mika Publishing, 1972.

MacKay, Donald. *Scotland Farewell: The People of the Hector*. Toronto: Mc Graw-Hill Ryerson, 1980.

MacKenzie, Alexander. *The History of the Highland Clearances*. Glasgow: P. J. Callaghan, 1883.

MacKenzie, A. A. "Antigonish Poor Farm and Asylum—Antigonish," in *Poverty, Poor Houses, and Philanthropy*. Project of Senior Scribes of Nova Scotia, Halifax: Senior Citizens' Secretariat, 1996.

MacKenzie, W.C. "The Social Life of the Community," in *Leabhar A'Chlachain, Home Life of the Highlanders, 1400-1746,* 38-51. Glasgow: Robert MacLehose, 1911.

MacKinnon, A. D. *The History of the Presbyterian Church in Cape Breton.* Antigonish: Formac, 1975.

MacKinnon, Charles. *The Scottish Highlanders.* New York: St. Martin's Press, 1984.

McLaren, George. *The Pictou Book: Stories of our Past.* New Glasgow, Nova Scotia: The Hector Publishing Company, 1954.

MacLean, Fitzroy. H*ighlanders: A History of the Scottish Clans.* London: David Campbell, 1995.

MacLean, Magnus. *The Literature of the Highlands.* London: Blackie and Sons, n.d.

MacLean, Raymond A. *Bishop John Cameron: Piety and Politics.* Antigonish: Casket Printing and Publishing Co., 1991.

MacLellan, Malcolm. *The Glen.* Antigonish: Casket Printing and Publishing Co., 1982.

MacLeod C. I. N. *Highland Scottish Folklore and Beliefs.* Antigonish: Formac, 1975.

————. *Stories from Nova Scotia.* Antigonish: Formac, 1974

MacNeil, Neil. *The Highland Heart in Nova Scotia.* New York: Charles Scribners Sons, 1948.

Martin, Martin. *A Description of the Western Isles of Scotland, 1716.* Stirling: Eneas MacKay, 1934. .

Martin, P. F., ed. *The Catholic Diocesan Directory of Nova Scotia.* Kentville: Kentville Publishing Co., 1936.

Moir, John S. *Enduring Witness: A History of the Presbyterian Church in Canada.* Toronto: Byrnt Press, 1975.

Munroe, M. N. "The Music of the Clans," in Leabhar A'Chlachain, *Home Life of the Highlanders, 1400-1746,* 110-22. Glasgow: Robert MacLehrose, 1911.

Patterson, George. *A History of Pictou County.* Pictou: Pictou Advocate, 1877.

————. *History of Victoria County.* Sydney, Nova Scotia: University College of Cape Breton Press,1985.

Pennant, Thomas. *A Tour in Scotland, MDCCLXXVI,* Part II. London: Benj. White, DCCLXXII.

Pierson, Ruth. R. "Women into the War Effort," in *The Politics of Diversity: Feminism, Marxism, and Nationalism,* edited by N. Roberta Hamilton and Michele Barrett,   101-35. Montreal: Book Center, 1987.

Polson, Alexander. *Our Highland Folklore Heritage.* Inverness: The Northern Chronicle Office, 1926.

Prebble, John. *Culloden.* Markham, Ontario: Penguin Books, 1967.

Rankin, D. J. *A History of the County of Antigonish, Nova Scotia.* Toronto: MacMillan Company of Canada, MCMXXIX.

Reid, W. Stanford. "The Scottish Presbyterian Tradition," in *The Scottish Tradition in Canada.* Edited by W. Stanford Reid, 118-36. Toronto: McClelland-Stewart, 1976.

Ross, Anne. *The Folklore of the Scottish Highlands.* London: B.T. Batsford, 1976.

Skene, W.F. *The Highlanders of Scotland.* Stirling: Eneas MacKay, 1902.

Stanley, Laurie. *The Well-Watered Garden: The Presbyterian Church in Cape Breton, 1798-1860.* Sydney, Nova Scotia: The University College of Cape Breton Press, 1983.

Stewart, David. *Sketches of the Character, Manners, and Present State of the Highlanders of Scotland.* Edinburgh: Longman, 1822.

Transactions of the Celtic Congress. Edited by D. R. Phillips. Report of the meetings held at Edinburgh, May 24-28. Perth: Milne, Tannahill, and Meuthen, 1920.

Urquhart Judy and Eric Ellington. *Eigg.* Edinburgh: Canongate Publishers, 1987.

The Xavieran Annual. Antigonish: Casket Printing, 1956.

Articles

Adams, Margaret I. "Highland Emigrations of 1788-1803." *The Scottish Historical Review* 17 (1920): 73-84.

Archibald, Mrs.Charles. "Early Scottish Settlers in Cape Breton." *Collections of the Nova Scotia Historical Society* xviii (1914): 69-100.

Beattie, Betsy. "Going Up to Lynn: Single Maritime Born Women in Lynn, Massasschusetts, 1879- 1930." *Acadiensis* 22, no. 1 (1992): 65-86.

Bland, M. S. "Henrietta the Homemaker and 'Rosie the Riveter': Images of Women in MacLean's Magazine, 1939-1950." *Atlantis* 8, no. 2 (Spring, 1983): 61-86.

Fergusson, Charles B. "Inaguration of the Free School System in Nova Scotia." *Journa lof Education* 14, no. 1 (1964): 3-28.

Geller, Gloria. "The Wartime Elections Act of 1917 and the Canadian Women's Movement." *Atlantis* 2, no. 1 (Autumn, 1976): 88-106.

Guilford, Janet. "Separate Spheres: The Feminization of Public School Teaching in Nova Scotia, 1838-1880." *Acadiensis* 22, no. 1 (1992): 44-64.

Keddy, Barbara, Mary LeDrew, Bonny Thompson, Liz Novaczek, Margie Stewart and Ruth Englehart. "The Nurse as Mother Surrogate: Oral Histories of Nova Scotia Nurses from the 1920s and the 1930s." *Health Care for Women International* 5, no. 4 (1984): 181-92.

MacArthur, Dugald, "Some Emigrant Ships from the Western Highlands," *Transactions of the Gaelic Society of Inverness* LV (1986-88): 324-45.

MacDonald, Alex (Gleannach), "The Part of Music in the Home Life of the Olden-time Gaels." *Transactions of the Gaelic Society of Inverness* XXXIII (1925-27): 122-46.

Mitchinson, Wendy. "Canadian Women and Church Missionary Societies in the Nineteenth Century: A Step Towards Independence," *Atlantis* 2, no. 2 (Spring, 1977): 57-75.

Moffatt, H. P. "One Hundred Years of Free Schools." *Journal of Education* 14, no. 1 (1964): 29-41.

Morton, Suzanne. "Older Women and Their Place in Nova Scotia, 1881-1931." *Atlantis* 20, no. 1 (Fall-Winter, 1995): 21-32.

Muise, D. A. "The Industrial Context of Inequality: Female Participation in Nova Scotia's Paid Labor Force, 1871-1921." *Acadiensis* 20, no. 1 (Spring, 1991), 3-31.

Murchison, T. M. "Highland Life as Reflected in Gaelic Literature." *Transactions of the Gaelic Society of Inverness* XXXVIII (1937-41): 217-42.

MacDonald, Colin S. "Early Highland Emigration to Nova Scotia and Prince Edward Island from 1770 to 1853." *Collections of the Nova Scotia Historical Society* 23 (1936): 41-48.

MacDonald, Colin. S. "West Highland Emigrants in Eastern Nova Scotia." *Collections of the Nova Scotia Historical Society* 32 (1959): 1-30.

MacNeil, Alan. "Scottish Settlement in Colonial Nova Scotia: A Case Study of St. Andrew's Township." *Scottish Tradition* 19 (1994): 60-79.

Thorton, Patricia A. "The Problem of Outmigration from Atlantic Canada, 1871-1921: A New Look." *Acadiensis* 15, no. 1 (Autumn, 1985): 3-34.

Government Documents

"Annual Report of the Superintendent of Education of Nova Scotia." For the year ending July 31, 1908, By A.H. MacKay. Halifax: King's Printer, 1909.

Canada. Report of the Commission Appointed under Order in Council, 1923, *The Industrial Unrest among the Steel Workers at Sydney, Nova Scotia* Printed as a Supplement to *The Labour Gazette,* February, 1924.

Canada. *Report of the Royal Commission Respecting the Coal Mines of the Povince of Nova Scotia, 1925* Ottawa: Kings Printers, 1926.

Canada. *Report of the Royal Commission on Coal,* 1946 Ottawa: King's Printers, 1947.

Canada. Royal Commission on Canada's Economic Prospects, *The Nova Scotia Coal Industry* Ottawa: Urwick, Currie, 1956.

Canada. Royal Commission on Health Services, 1964. *Nursing Education in Canada.* By H.K. Mussallem. Ottawa: Queen's Printer, 1965.

Canada. Royal Commission on Health Services, *Sociological Factors Affecting Recruitment in the Nursing Profession* By R. A. H. Robson. Ottawa: Queen's Printers, 1967.

Dominion Bureau of Statistics. "Agriculture,"*Seventh Census of Canada,* 1931. 3 Ottawa: King's Printers, 1936.

Journal of Proceedings of the House of Assembly of the Province of Nova Scotia. Session 1899. Halifax: William MacNab, 1899.

Journal of Proceedings of the House of Assembly of the Province of Nova Scotia. Appendix No. 8,"Agriculture,"Halifax: McAlpine, 1900.

Nova Scotia."Annual Report of the Superintendent of Education, Appendix No. 5."*Journal of Education,* 1884.

Nova Scotia, *Journal of the Proceedings of the House of Assembly*, Appendix No. 3,"Public Charities,"Halifax: McAlpine Publishers, 1900.

Nova Scotia, Antigonish County. *A Study of Land Ulilization, Farm Production and Rural Living Nova Scotia Department of Agriculture,* Bulletin No. 118, January, 1936.

Nova Scotia. *Report of the Royal Commission on Public School Finances in Nova Scotia* By V. J. Pottier, Commissioner. Halifax: Queen's Printer, 1954.

Nova Scotia. Department of Public Welfare. *The Development of Social Welfare in Nova Scotia* 1967.

Nova Scotia."Report of the Royal Commission on Education, Public Service and Provincial-Municipal Relations." *Summary and Recommendations* Halifax: Queen's Printer, 1974.

Nova Scotia. *Royal Commission: Provincial Economic Inquiry.* Halifax: King's Printers, 1934.

Revised Statutes of Nova Scotia. 1 Halifax: King's Printers, 1923.

Newspapers

Folia Montana
The Casket
The Cape Breton Mirror
The Cape Breton Post

The Eastern Chronicle
The Halifax Herald
The Inverness News
The Mail Star
The Inverness Courier

Magazines

"Departure of an Emigrant Ship,"*The Celtic Magazine,* ix, xcviii., November, 1883.

"St. Mary's Infant Home, Sydney," *Little Flower Messenger*, 1928.

Theses and Dissertations

Frank, D. A."The Cape Breton Coal Miners, 1917-1926."PhD diss., Dalhousie University, 1979.

MacGillivray, Donald."Industrial Unrest in Cape Breton, 1919-1925."MA Thesis, University of New Brunswick, 1971.

Somers, Mary."The Little Flower Institute,"MA Thesis, Catholic University of America, 1933.

Papers Read at Meetings

Butts, Peggy."Pilgrimage from France to Montreal to Antigonish: Living the Visitation Mystery of the Virgin Mary."Paper presented at the Reverend A. A.Johnston Memorial Conference. Antigonish, Nova Scotia, August 19-20, 1994.

Cameron, C. S."The Iron and Steel Industry in Canada."London: Cleveland House, 1925. Reprinted from the proceedings of the Empire Mining and Metallurgical Congress.

Fultz, Joan."The Marthas: A Story of Pioneering Faith."Paper presented to the Rev. A. A. Johnston Memorial Conference, Antigonish, Nova Scotia, August 19-20, 1994.

Guilford, Janet."Family Strategies and Professional Careers: The Experience of Women Teachers in Nineteenth Century Nova Scotia."Invited lecture in the Dawson Lecture Series, Nova Scotia Teachers College, Truro, Nova Scotia, 1994.

MacDonnell, Margaret."The Contribution of the Congregation de Notre Dame to the Scottish Gaelic 'Renaissance' in Nova Scotia."Paper delivered to the Canadian Association for Scottish Studies, Fredericton, New Brunswick, June 2, 1977.

McKenna, M. Olga. "The Sisters of Charity, Halifax: Their Legacy of Service to the Diocese of Antigonish, 1882-1994." Paper presented at the Reverend A. A. Johnston Memorial Conference, St. Francis Xavier University, August 19-20, 1994.

Sinclair, D. "Highland Emigration to Nova Scotia." Paper presented to the Nova Scotia Historical Society. Reprinted in *The Casket*, 9 September, 1943.

Pamphlets and Reports

Alexander, Laurie, *A Preliminary Review of the History of Coal Mining in Nova Scotia*, Research Report. Nova Scotia Museum of Industry, 1990.

Annals, Holy Angels Convent, 1885-1921, Beaton Institute.

Annals, Mount St. Bernard, 1917, reproduced in "Origin of the Congregation de Notre Dame," Provincial Archives, CNDs.

Annals, Bethany, 1958, Bethany Archives.

Annals, Hamilton Memorial Hospital, 1937-1938, Archives, Motherhouse, Sisters of Charity.

Biographical Sketch of Mother Ignatius, Bethany Archives, n.d.

The Board of Temperance and Moral Reform of the Methodist Church and the Board of Social Services and Evangelism of the Presbyterian Church, *Sydney, Nova Scotia: The report of a Brief Investigation of Social Conditions in the City*, Beaton Institute, n.d.

Calendars of St. Francis Xavier College, 1890s.

Campbell, M. R., "The History of Basic Steel Maunfacturing at Sydney, Nova Scotia," *Transactions*, Vol. 55, Annual Meeting, Mining Society of Nova Scotia, July, 1952, Nova Scotia Museum of Industry.

Congregation de Notre Dame in the Maritimes, Provincial Archives, CNDs.

Family Service Bureau: St. Theresa's Parish, Sydney, Archives, Bethany.

Earle, M. *A Preliminary Review of Nova Scotia's Historical Economic Context, 1920-1980*, Halifax: Beach Meadows Research Associates, 1992.

Earle, M. *A Preliminary Report on Unionization and Strikes in Nova Scotia, 1880-1980*, Research Report, Nova Scotia Museum of Industry, 1993.

Fergusson, C. B., ed., *Uniake's Sketches of Cape Breton and Other papers Relating to Cape Breton Island*, Public Archives of Nova Scotia, 1958.

Forsey, Eugene. *Economic and Social aspects of the Nova Scotia Coal Industry*, Nova Scotia Museum of Industry, 1948.

A General View of Religious Life, Archives, Bethany.

One Hundred Years of Christian Education, St. Joseph's Convent, Mabou, 1887-1987, Provincial Archives, CNDs.

History of Stella Maris Convent, Provincial Archives, CNDs.

Kirincich, M. S. *Our Lady of Lourdes Church, 1883-1983,* Archives, Motherhouse, Sisters of Charity.

Little Flower Institute: Historical Highlights, Archives, Bethany, n.d.

Lyons, Claire M. *History of Nursing Education in Nova Scotia,* Archives, Bethany.

MacSween, D., *Coal Mining in Cape Breton,* Report on Coal, Beaton Institute, n.d.

MacMahon, M., *St. Martha's School of Nursing,* Archives, Bethany, 1995.

Mount St. Bernard Centennial, 1883-1983, Provincial Archives, CNDs.

Martell, J.S., *Immigration to and Emigration from Nova Scotia, 1815-1838,* Public Archives of Nova Scotia, Publication No. 6. 1942.

Murray, Janice, *Relief and Charity to Immigrants in Cape Breton, 1820-1850,* Ethnic Report, Beaton Institute, 1984.

Nilsen, K. E. "The Nova Scotia Gael in Boston," *Proceedings of the Harvard Celtic Colloquium,* Vol. 6, 1986.

Notes on the Founding and Growth of the Margaree Forks School, Archives, Bethany.

O'Grady, Brendan, *A Century in Education: The Congregation of Notre Dame in Prince Edward Island, 1873-1973,"* Provincial Archives, C.N.D.

Plessis, Bp. Joseph-Octave, *The Plessis Diary of 1811 and 1812,* Translated into English by Arthur LeBlanc and Angus A. Johnston, 1954.

Ryan, Judith. *History of Women in Office Work in Nova Scotia,* Research Report, Nova Scotia Museum of Industry, 1992.

———. *Electrification of Nova Scotia Homes,* Research Report. Nova Scotia Museum of Industry, 1993.

———. *Women's Unpaid Work: A Case Study of Coal Miners' Wives and Widows,* Research Report, Nova Scotia Museum of Industry, 1993.

Historical Perspective on Nursing Education, RNANS Entry to Practice Committee.

St. Anne's Parish, 1866- 1966, Glace Bay: Brodie printing, 1967.

St. Mary's Hospital, 1925-1977, Archives, Bethany.

Whidden, D. G., *The History of the Town of Antigonish,* 1934, Special Collections, St. Francis Xavier University.

Wylie, William T., *Coal Culture: The History and Commemoration of Coal Mining in Nova Scotia*, Coal Report, Historic Sites and Monuments Board of Canada, 1997.

Index

MEMBER OF SCABRINI GROUP

Québec, Canada
2006